Winnipeg, Manitoba, Canada Book 5 in Colour Photos, Saving Our History One Photo at a Time

Photography
by Barbara Raué
2016

Series Name:
Cruising Canada

Book 5: Winnipeg, Manitoba Book 5

Cover photo: 222 Broadway Avenue, Hotel Fort Garry,
Page 29

The Authority on Saving Our History One Photo at a Time in colour photos
Series Name: Cruising Canada

Books 1-9: Winnipeg, Manitoba

Series Name: Cruising Ontario

Books Available in Alphabetical Order:
Aberfoyle, Acton, Alton, Amherstburg, Ancaster, Arthur, Aylmer, Ayr, Belleville, Bloomingdale, Brantford, Brockville, Burlington, Caledon, Caledonia, Cambridge, Clifford, Conestogo, Cornwall, Delhi, Dorchester to Aylmer, Drayton, Drumbo, Dundas, Eden Mills, Elmira, Elora, Erin, Essex, Fergus, Goderich, Guelph, Hagersville, Hamilton, Hanover, Harriston, Hespeler, Jarvis, Kemptville, Kingston, Kingsville, Kitchener, Linwood, Listowel, London, Lucknow, Mariatown to Maitland, Merrickville, Midland, Mono, Morrisburg, Mount Forest, Neustadt, New Hamburg, Newboro, Niagara-on-the-Lake, Oakville, Orangeville, Orillia, Ottawa, Owen Sound, Palmerston, Penetanguishene, Perth, Peterborough, Petrolia, Port Elgin, Portland, Preston, Smiths Falls, Rockwood, Sarnia, Seaforth, Sheffield, Shelburne, Simcoe, Southampton, St. Jacobs, St. Marys, St. Thomas, Stoney Creek, Stratford, Thamesford, Tillsonburg, Waterdown, Waterford, Waterloo, Welland, Wellesley, Westport, Windsor, Wingham, Woodstock

Other Books by Barbara Raue

Coins of Gold

Arrows, Indians and Love

The Life and Times of Barbara
Volume 1: Inventions That Have Enhanced My Life
Volume 2: Entertainment That I Have Enjoyed
Volume 3: East Coast Trips
Volume 4: Olympics Have Always Intrigued Me
Volume 5: Wonders of the World
Volume 6: Caribbean Cruises We Have Enjoyed
Volume 7: Animals
Volume 8: Storms and Other Major Disasters in My Lifetime
Volume 9: Wars, Terrorist Attacks and Major Disasters

The Cromwell Family Book

Laura Secord Discovered

Daddy Where Are You?

Montana Series
Book 1: Montana Dream
Book 2: Life on the Montana Frontier
Book 3: Montana to Boston and Back
Book 4: Montana Sons Go to War
Book 5: Montana Sons Return From War

Visit Barbara's website to view all of her books
http://barbararaue.ca

Table of Contents

Winnipeg is located at the confluence of two rivers, the Assiniboine River and the Red River. The city sits amidst a vast flatland surrounded by hundreds of parks and lakes.

The capital city of the Canadian province of Manitoba, Winnipeg has survived battles, uprisings and floods. It has come a long way since its days as a community of trading posts to become one of the most diversified economies in Canada. The city has a number of heritage sites which have earned it the title of Cultural Capital of Canada.

One of the most loved fictional characters, Winnie-the-Pooh originated in Winnipeg. In 1914 an orphaned bear cub stole the heart of Canadian Lieutenant Coleburn, who bought it for $20 from a hunter who had shot the cub's mother. The cub was named Winnipeg and became the regimental mascot. When Coleburn travelled to Europe during World War I he smuggled "Winnie" into London, England. He left the bear at the London Zoo to avoid the stress of taking the cub back to Canada. A short time later English author A.A. Milne saw Winnipeg during a visit to the zoo and was struck by the cub's personality. Winnipeg the cub was Milne's inspiration for the creation of the character called WINNIE-THE-POOH. The statue of Winnipeg, the bear cub and Lieutenant Coleburn, can be found in Assiniboine Park, Winnipeg.

Academy Road runs from Maryland Bridge to Wellington Crescent, and intersects with Wellington. This is Winnipeg's business improvement zone and also one of the most exclusive districts in Winnipeg. This is where you can find exclusive designer boutiques, specialty food shops, luxury bath and beauty products, European fashions and footwear, among other things.

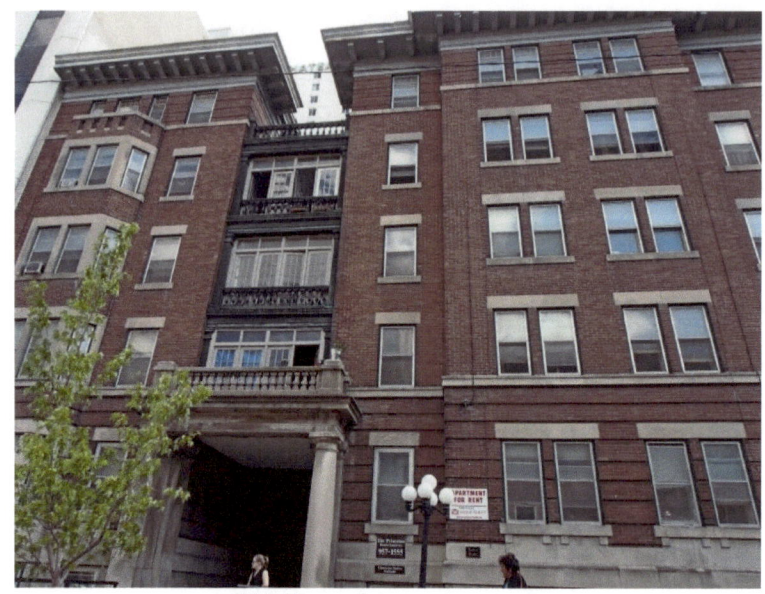

314 Broadway Avenue

The Princeton Apartments, architect William Wallace Blair, built in 1909 of reinforced concrete and brick, is a five-storey residential structure. Its W-shaped plan, intended to maximize available natural light and ventilation, and dignified Beaux-Arts Classical styling are rare among the city's historic apartment blocks. Key exterior elements that define the block's stately style and residential function include its multi-storey bay windows, the front cladding of rusticated stone (base) and red pressed brick (upper walls) with generous stone ornamentation. The imposing, classically adorned front is symmetrical and column-like. The grand twin entranceways into the main wells feature stone frontispieces of Tuscan columns, plain entablatures, and elegant balustrades and attached pilasters. The windows are mostly tall rectangles in singles or groups of two or more, including four-storey bay windows. The details include the massive stone and metal entablature complete with a modillioned cornice, the stone-capped brick parapet, and the stone-capped battlements atop the front bay windows.

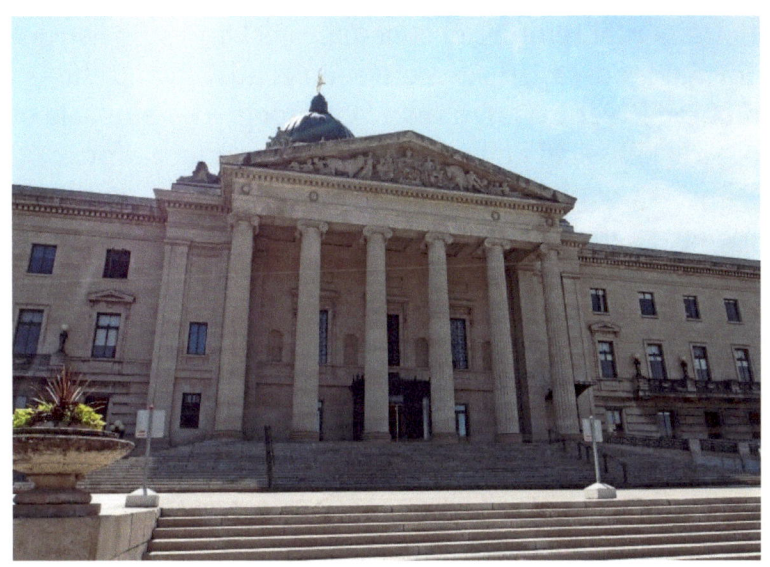

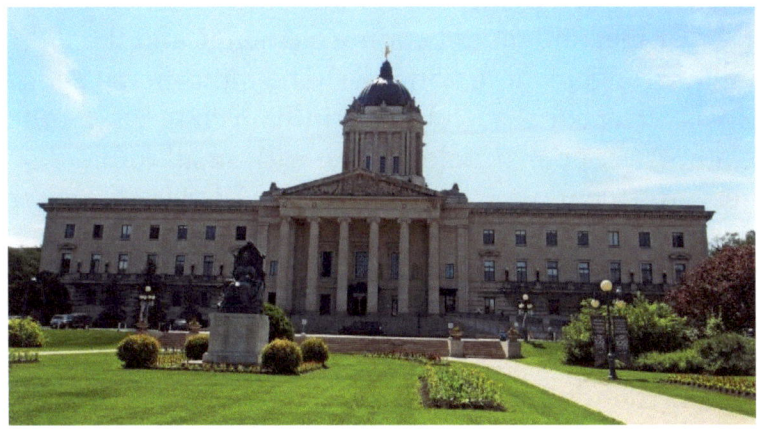

450 Broadway Avenue – Manitoba Legislative Building

The Manitoba Legislative Building, erected in 1913-20, is a monumental reinforced concrete, steel and stone structure on a formal landscaped site between Broadway and the Assiniboine River in downtown Winnipeg. The pinnacle of Beaux-Arts Classical architecture in the province is an imposing seat of government symbolic of local strength and vitality and of the import of the official functions that occur within its walls. The solid, massive edifice, which dominates its expansive site and is visible from various vantages, is a disciplined expression of classical Greek Revival styling crowned by a symbol of youth and enterprise, the Golden Boy, graced by allegorical and historical ornament, and proudly wrapped in local Tyndall limestone. Key elements that define the building's stately Beaux-Arts Classical architecture include the symmetrical H-shaped massing, rising three storeys from a high base, and sheathed in channeled and ashlar Tyndall stone. The strong horizontal lines are reinforced by the flat roof, continuous modillioned cornice, parapet and other banding elements, and the rhythmic arrangement of windows. The multi-tiered central tower has offset corners, fluted Corinthian columns, a full entablature, a copper-paneled dome with small round dormers, and a cupola crowned with the Golden Boy. There are porticoes on each façade, large stone staircases, and colonnades with giant order columns, full entablatures, pediments, and finely detailed entrances. There are many rectangular windows with some framed by architraves, others in relief surrounds. The exuberant and profuse details throughout include stone and metal balustrades, pilasters, engaged columns, belt courses, niches, raised panels, and urns. There are many exceptional historical and allegorical sculptures, including twin sphinxes flanking the north pediment, figures and groupings of figures.

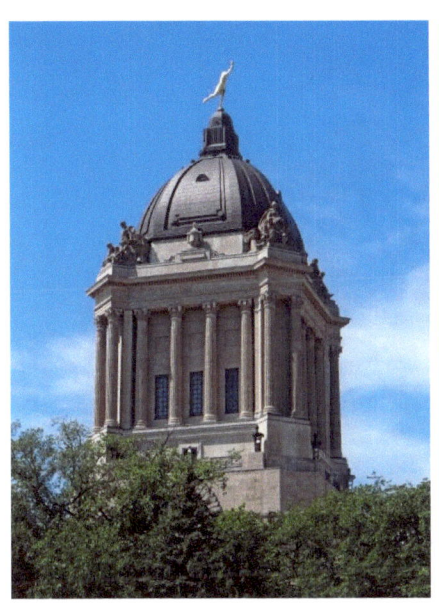
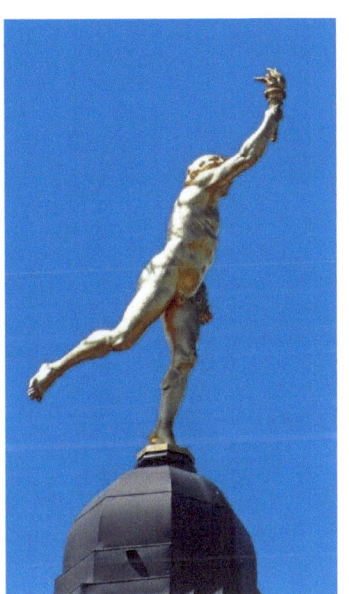
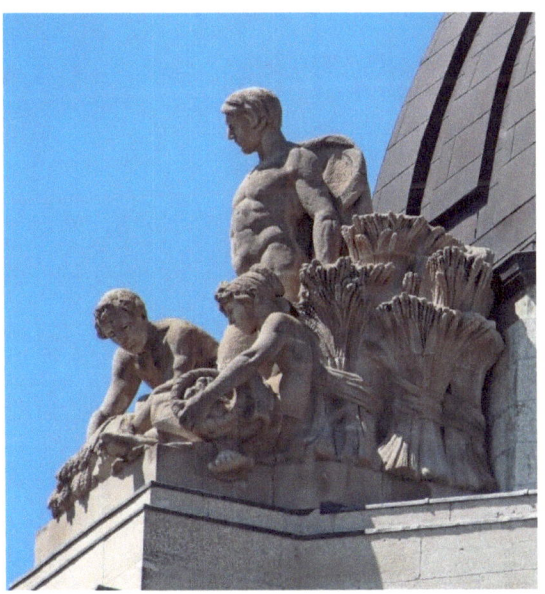

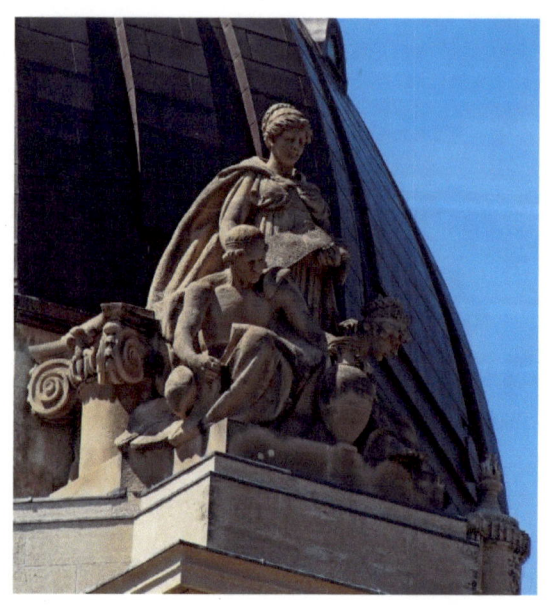

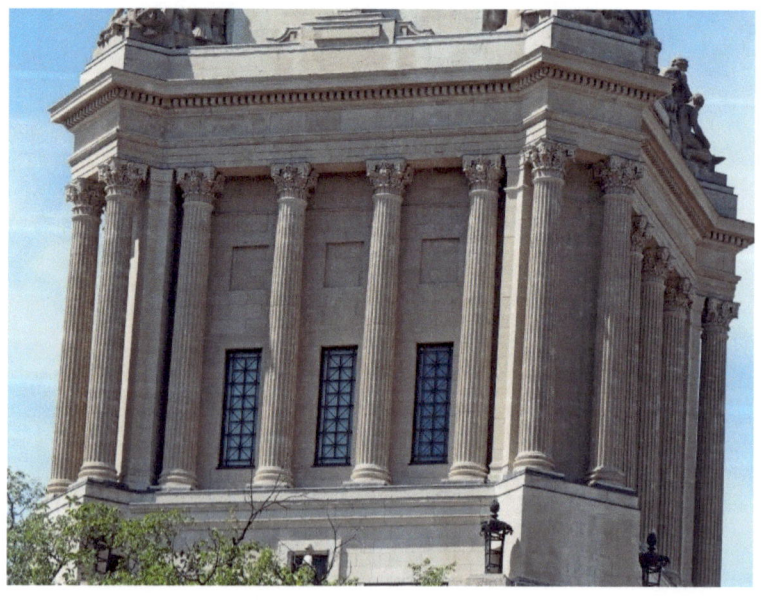

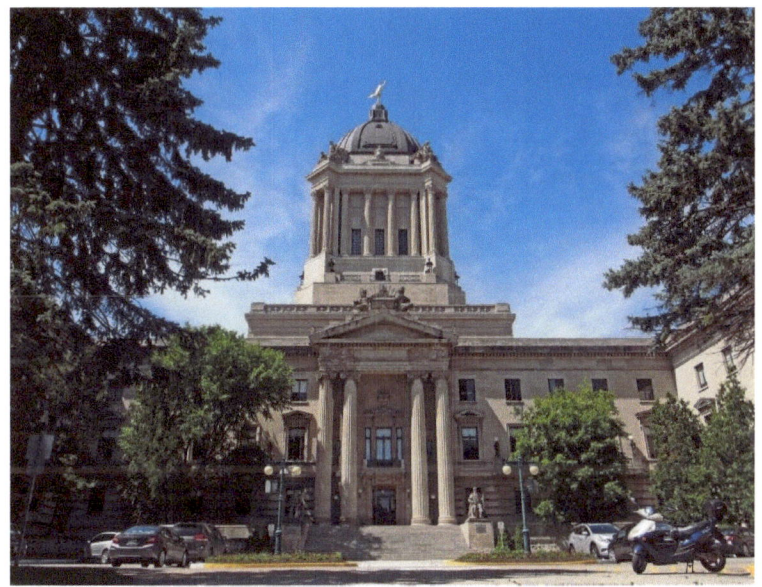

From Edmonton Street Side

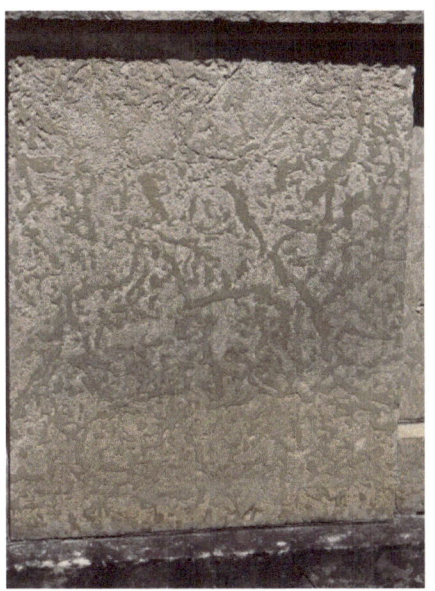

Marble with fossils

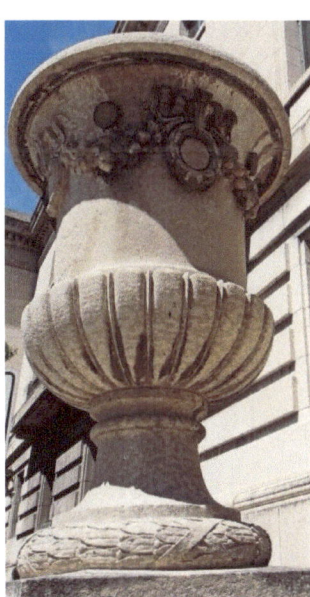

Large vase

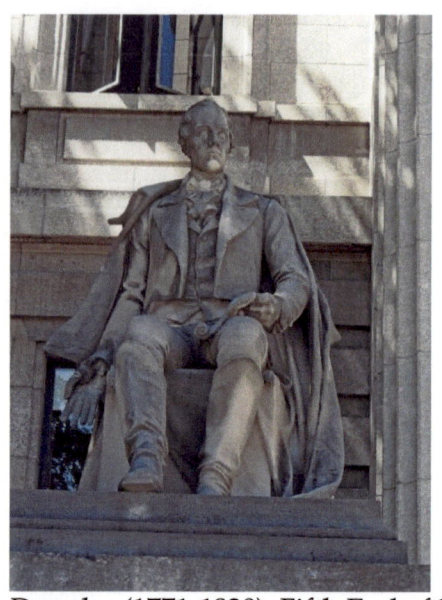

It was Thomas Douglas (1771-1820), Fifth Earl of Selkirk, whose inspired leadership and support attracted settlers in Scotland and Ireland to the settlement at the forks of the Red and Assiniboine Rivers with the first group arriving in August 1812.

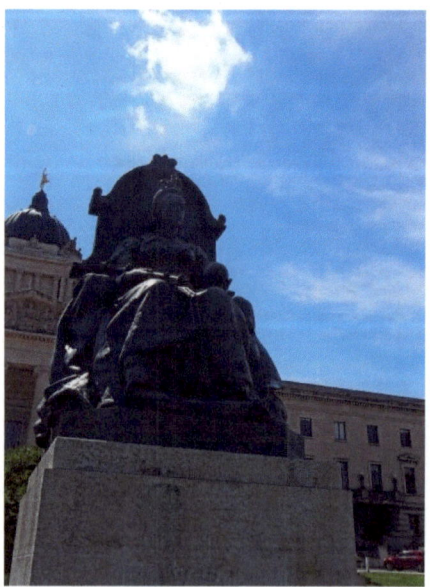

Queen Victoria 1837-1901

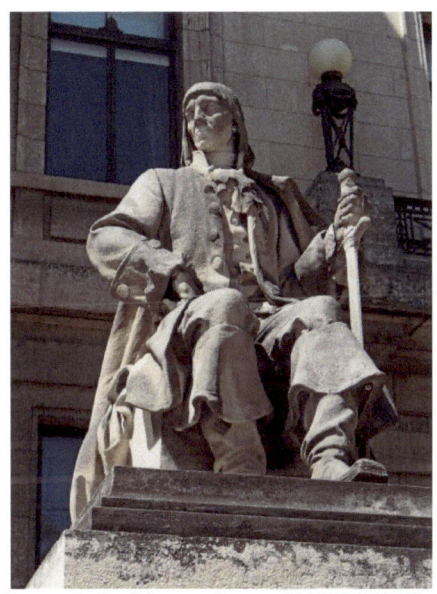

Pierre Gaultier, Sieur de la Verendrye, (1685-1749) was born in Canada. In search of the Western sea, he explored the central part of the North American continent to within sight of the Rocky Mountains. He reached the Red River at the Forks (Winnipeg) in 1738.

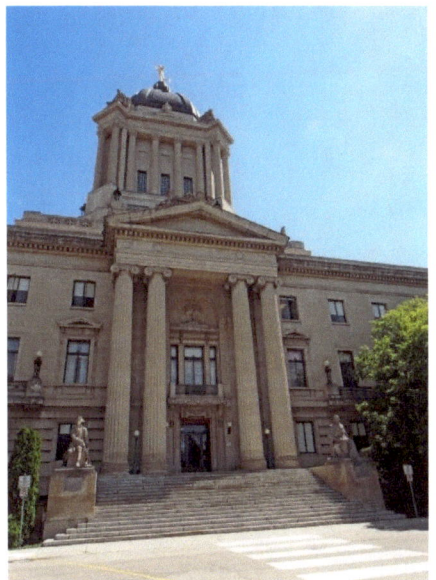

View from Osborne Street

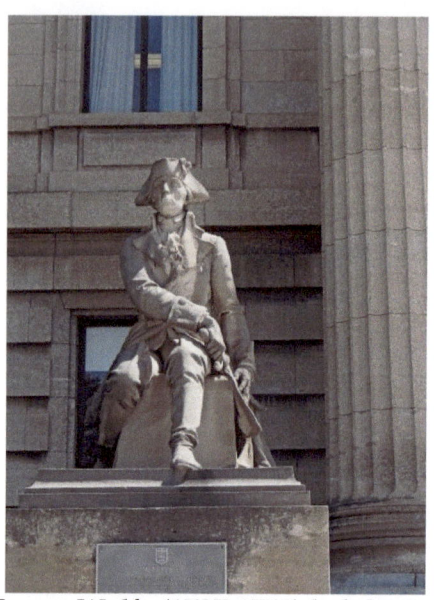

Major General James Wolfe (1727-1759) led the British forces and died in taking Quebec at the first Battle of the Plains of Abraham on September 13, 1759. Effective rule over Canada from France ended and cession of Canada to Great Britain was completed in 1763.

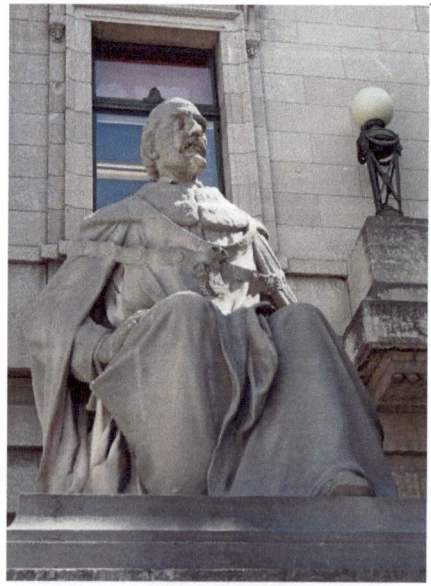

The Earl of Dufferin (1826-1902), Governor General of Canada from 1872-1878, was the first Vice-Regal representative to visit Manitoba.

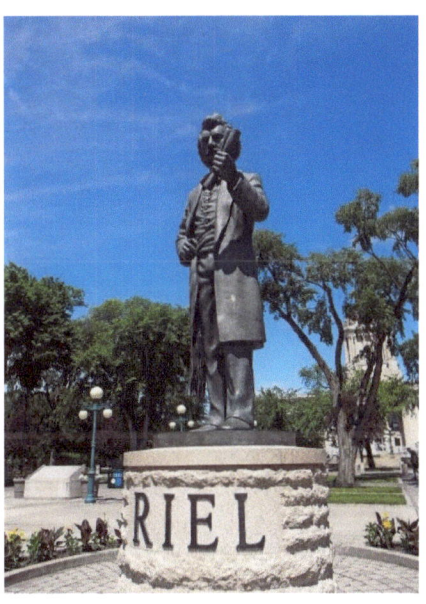

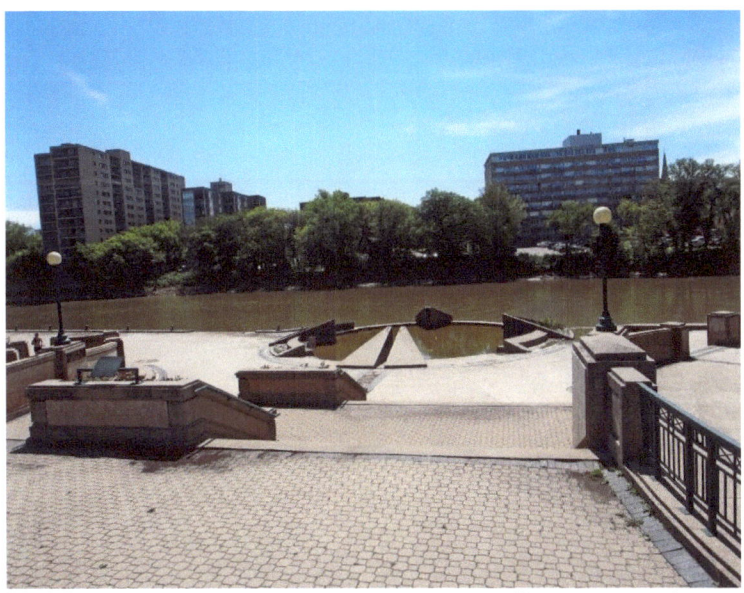

This section of the Assiniboine River Walkway provides an uninterrupted pedestrian path from the grounds of the Legislative Building to the Forks at the junction of the Red and Assiniboine Rivers.

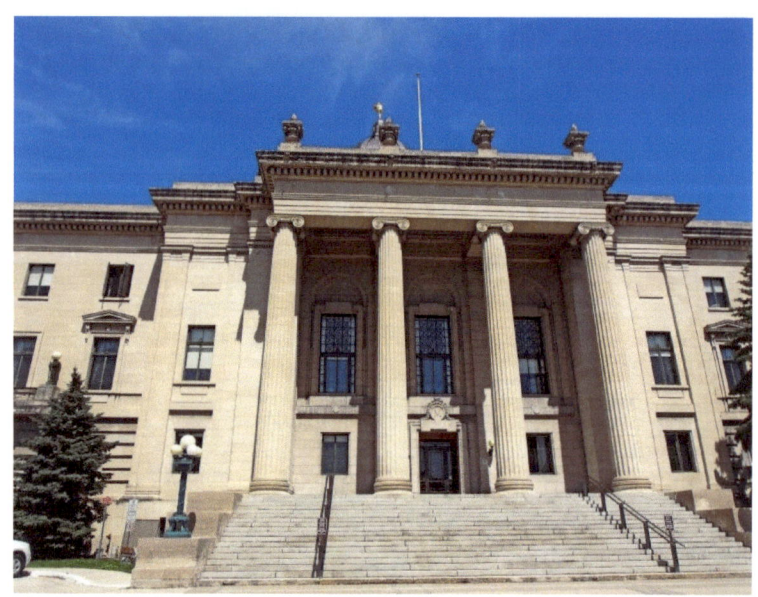

From rear

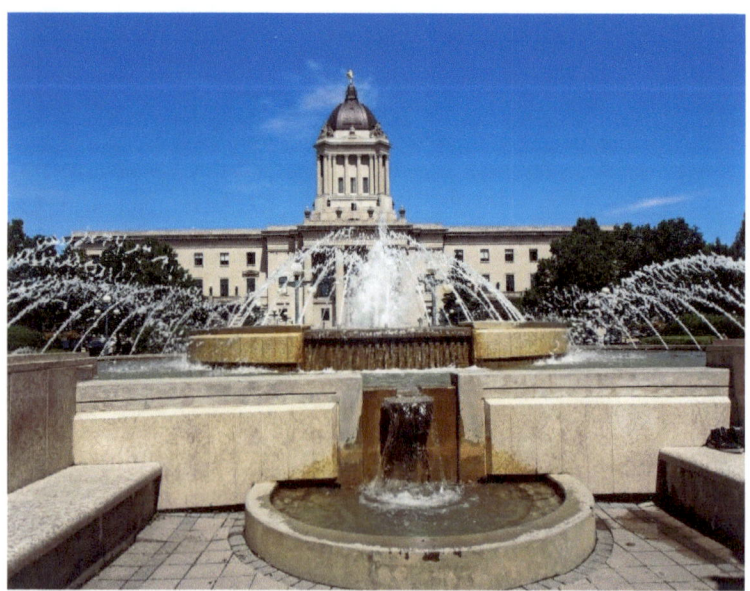

From Manitoba Plaza

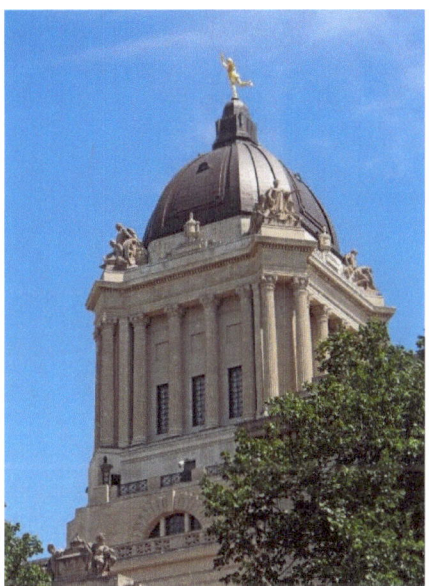

View from another angle

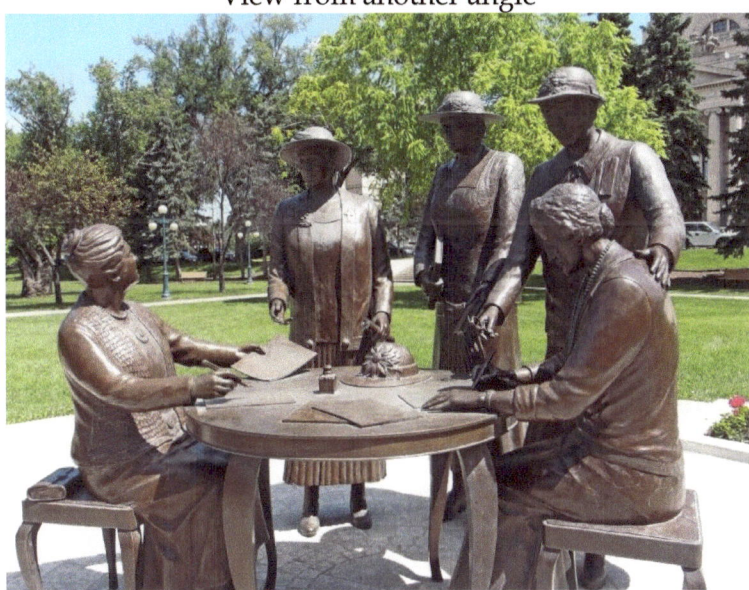

Nellie McClung (1873-1951) believed a few committed women could bring about change. On January 27, 1916, she helped Manitoba women become the first in Canada to win the right to vote. As part of the "Famous Five" shown here, she helped influence the 1929 decision for women to be recognized as "persons" under the British North America Act. From left: Henrietta Muir Edwards, Emily Murphy, Irene Parlby, Louise McKinney and Nellie McClung

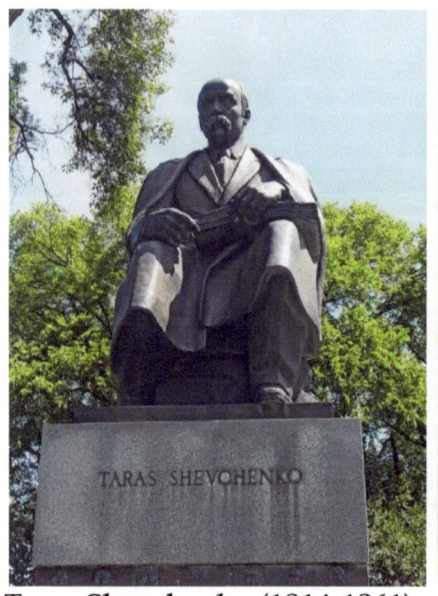
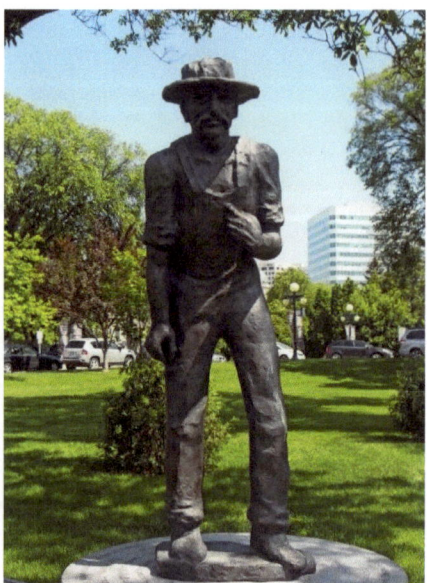

Taras Shevchenko (1814-1861)
National Poet of Ukraine,
Champion of Justice and
Freedom for all

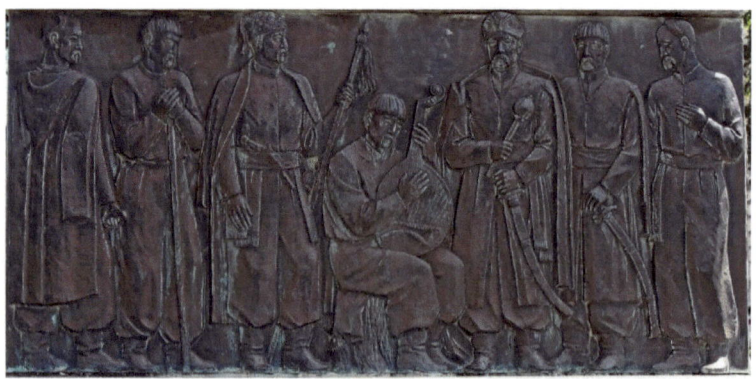

Thousands of Ukrainians and other Eastern Europeans were
unjustly imprisoned as "enemy aliens" during Canada's first
national internment operations of 1914-1920.

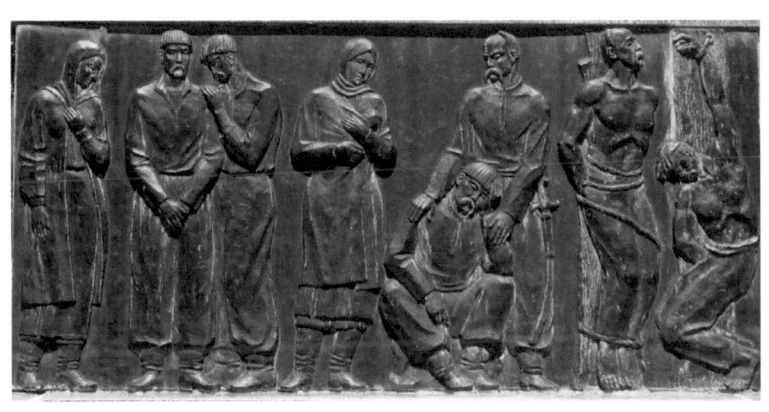

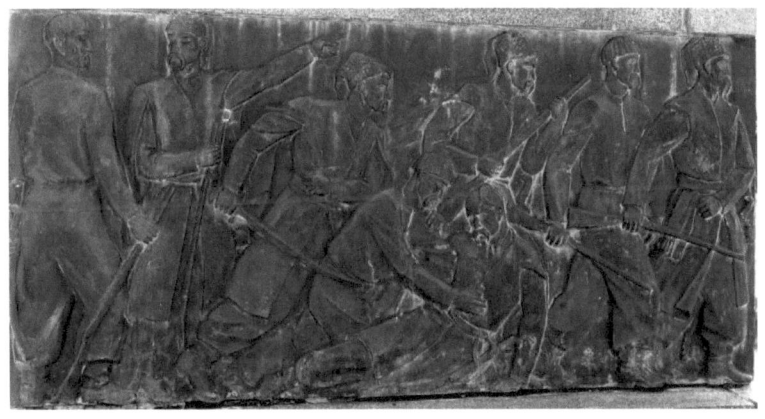

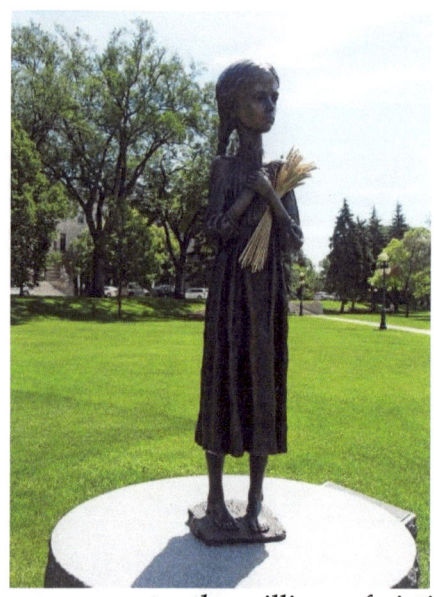

The monument commemorates the millions of victims of enforced starvation during the Holodomor Famine Genocide in Ukraine 1932-1933. Many survivors emigrated to Canada and settled in Manitoba where they could live in peace and freedom.

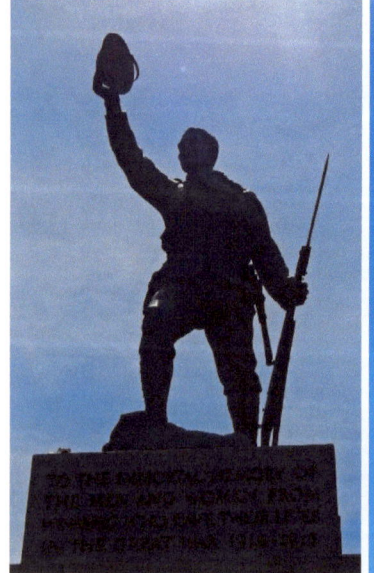
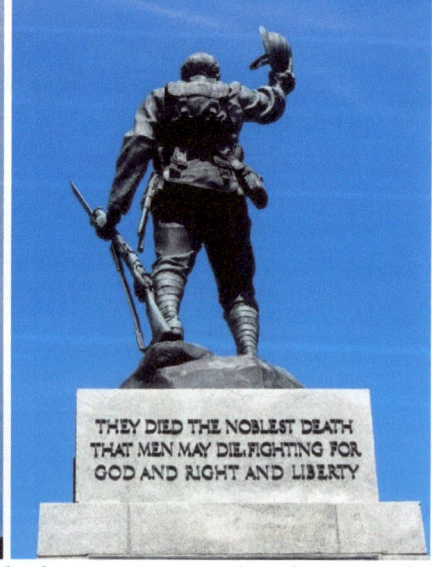

They died the noblest death that men may die, fighting for God and right and liberty (1914-1918)

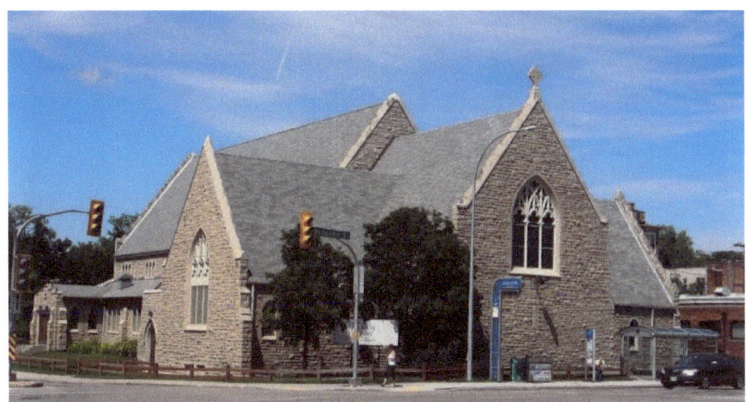

499 Broadway Avenue at corner of Osborne - All Saints
Anglican Church – stone English Gothic Revival

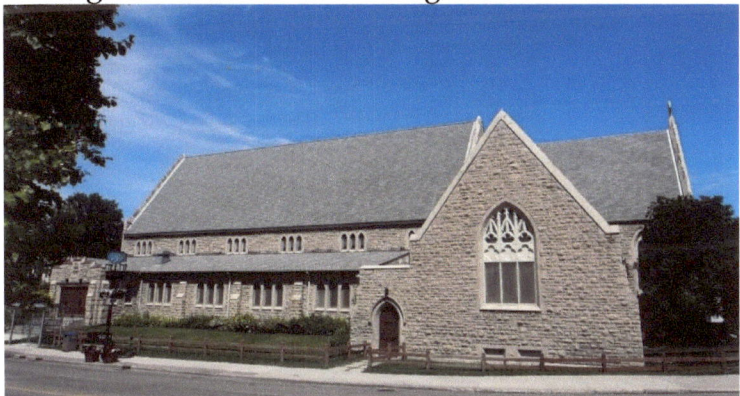

All Saints' Anglican Church has stood at the corner of Broadway and
Osborne Street North since 1884, the original building being made of
wood, designed in an English neo-Gothic style and capable of seating 450
people. The widening of Osborne Street North in the 1920s led to this
building's demolition and the erection of the 1925-26 church. In 1952, a
connecting building was constructed between the church and the original
parish hall. In 1964, architect George Stewart designed a new church
parish hall. This section of the All Saints' Anglican Church complex is sited
on the corner of Broadway Avenue and Colony Street. The main (Colony
Street) and south (Broadway) elevations are faced in rough-hewn Tyndall
stone, a pattern echoing that of the adjacent Tyndall stone neo-Gothic
church erected 29 years earlier. The parish hall's rectangular bulk is broken
up by a series of narrow windows, which are separated with light-toned

concrete cross-shaped mullions. With pointed vertical ends, these mullions draw the eye upward, a gesture which recalls the neo-Gothic treatment of the earlier church reimagined in a modernist vein. The rear of the hall is finished in stucco, with Tyndall stone sills and galvanized metal trim.

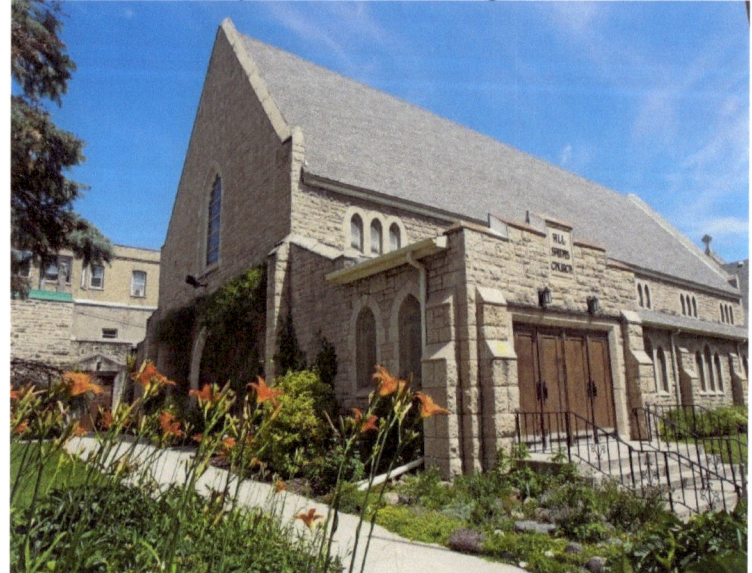

175 Colony Street – Parish Hall

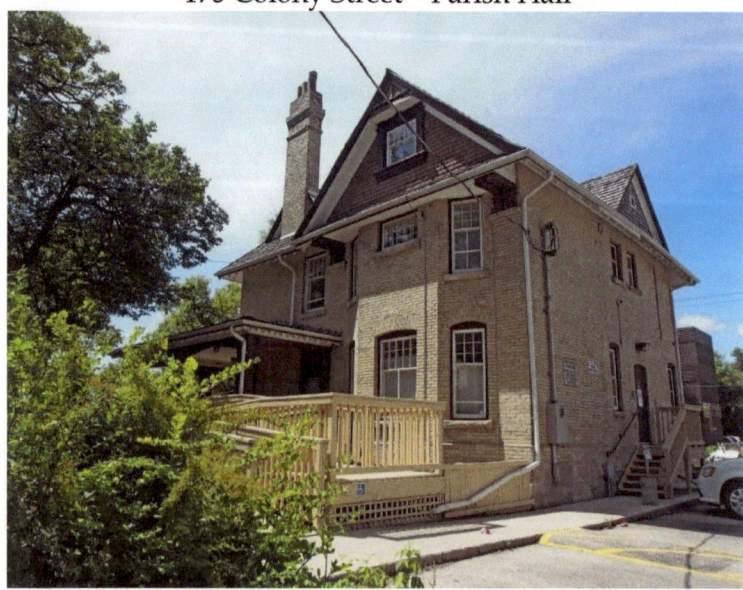

Colony Street – tall chimney

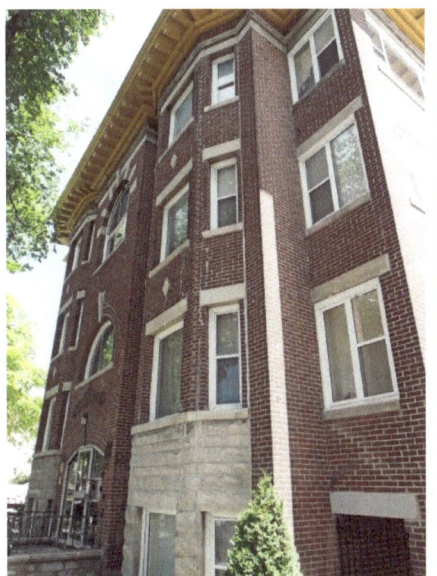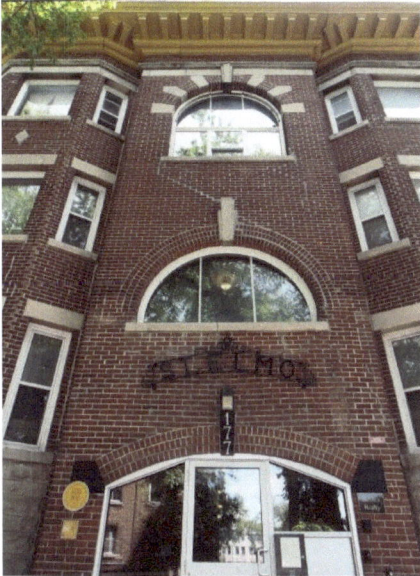

177 Colony Street - St. Elmo Apartments – 1910 - This picturesque three-storey heritage apartment building provides a quiet atmosphere in a convenient and quiet location. It has a central corridor plan in Neo-Georgian style, although the cornice work and brackets are more typical of the Queen Anne style. The street façade has contrasting red brick and light-colored concrete lintels, while the rear of the building is common sand brick colored with no decoration.

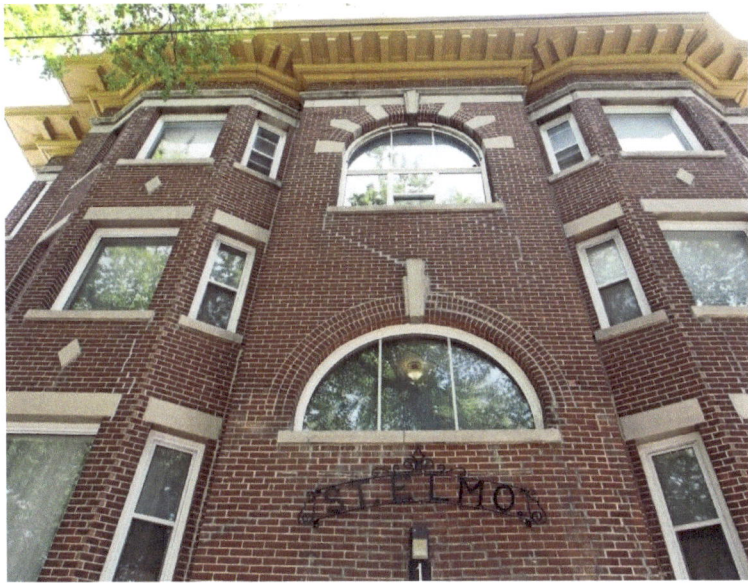

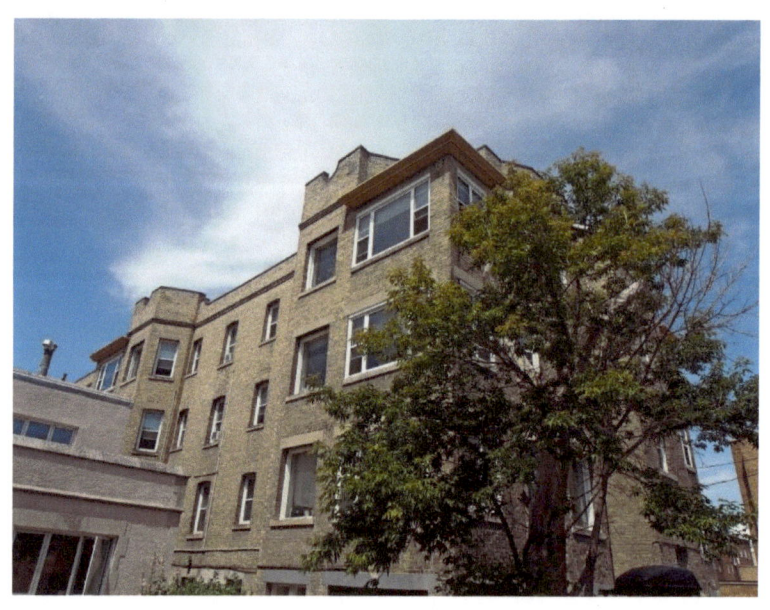

Rear of 177 Colony Street

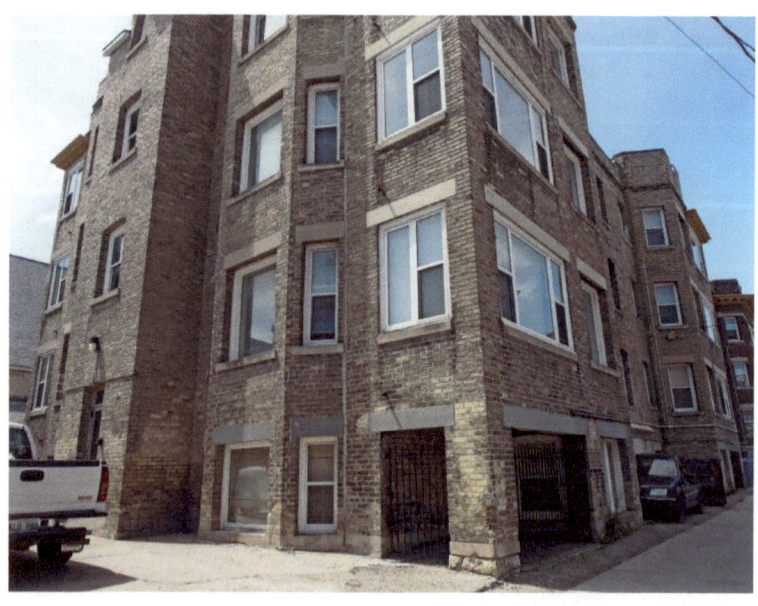

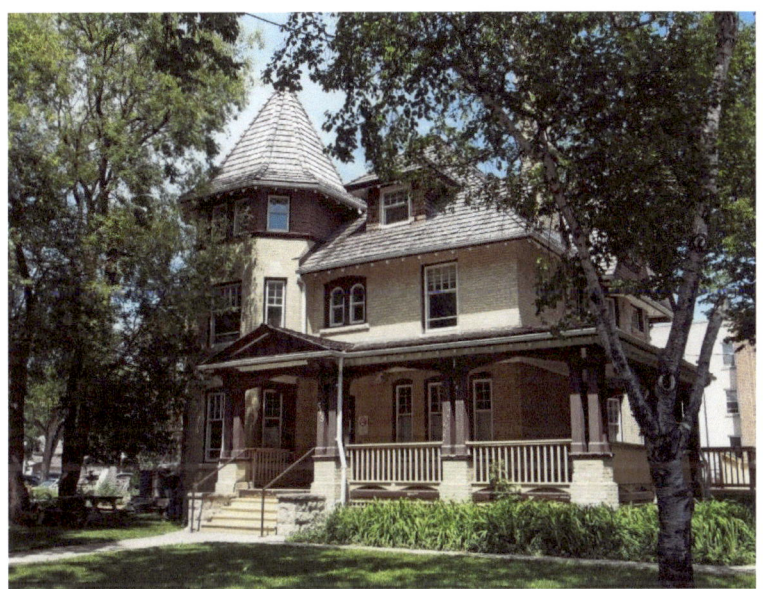

545 Broadway Avenue – three-storey tower with cone-shaped roof, dormer, pediment, deep wraparound verandah

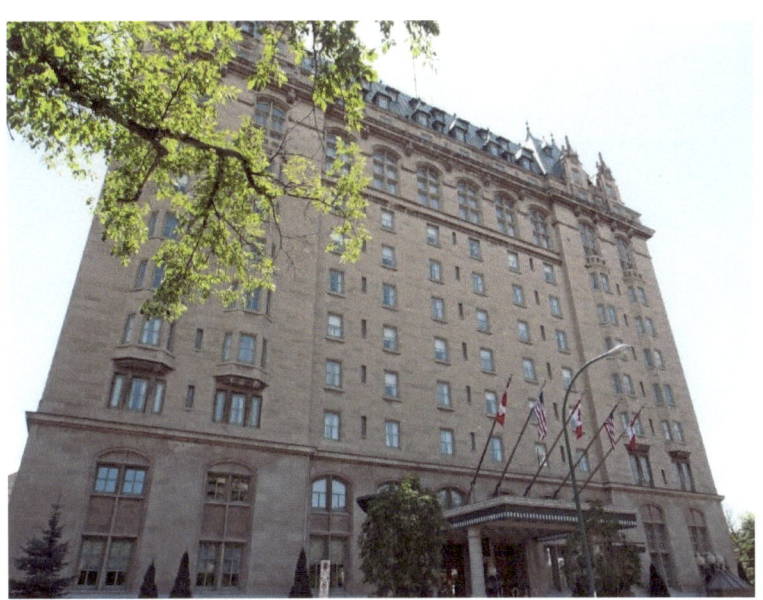

222 Broadway Avenue – Hotel Fort Garry

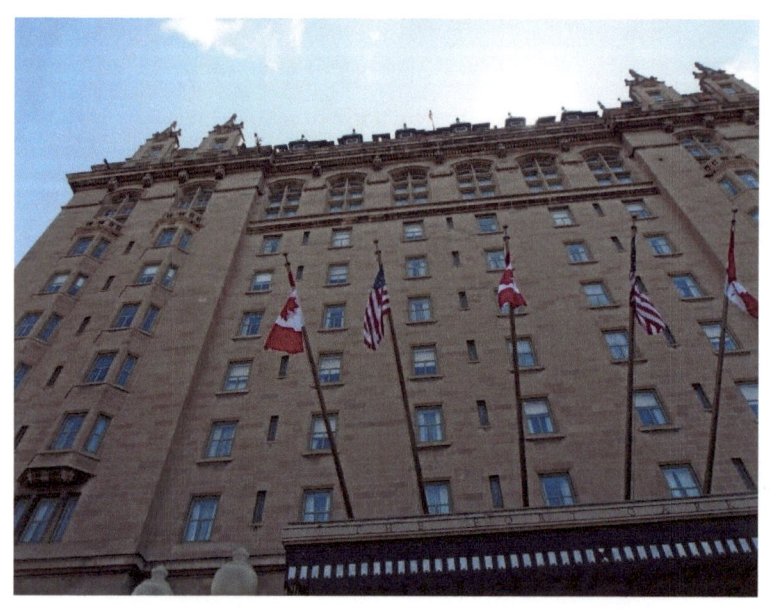

222 Broadway Avenue – Hotel Fort Garry

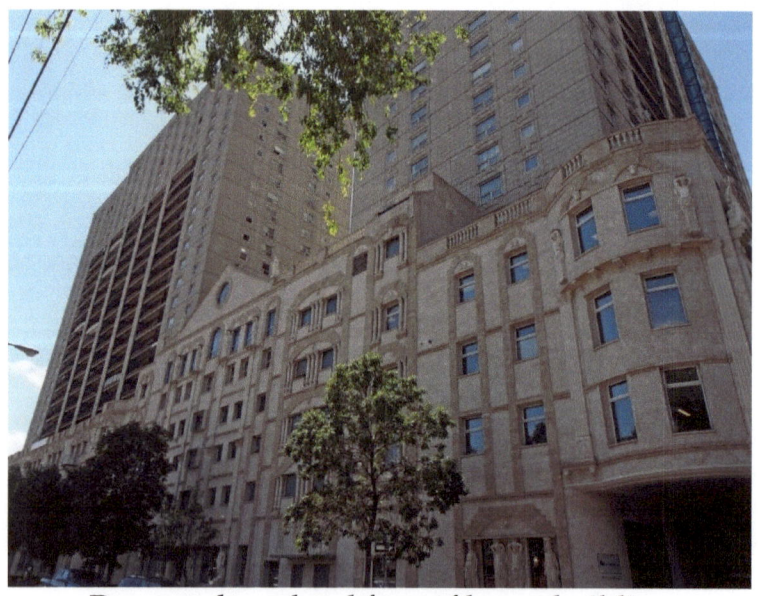

Parapet above level four of lower building

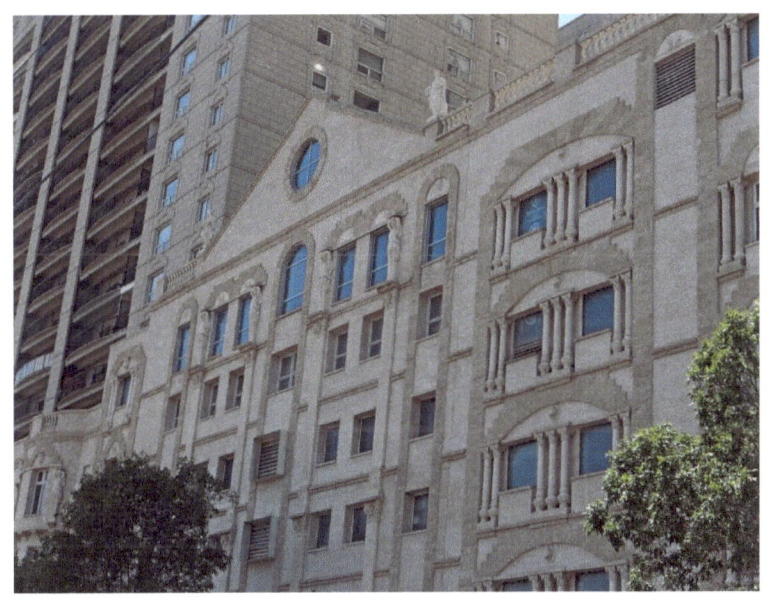

222 Broadway Avenue – Hotel Fort Garry

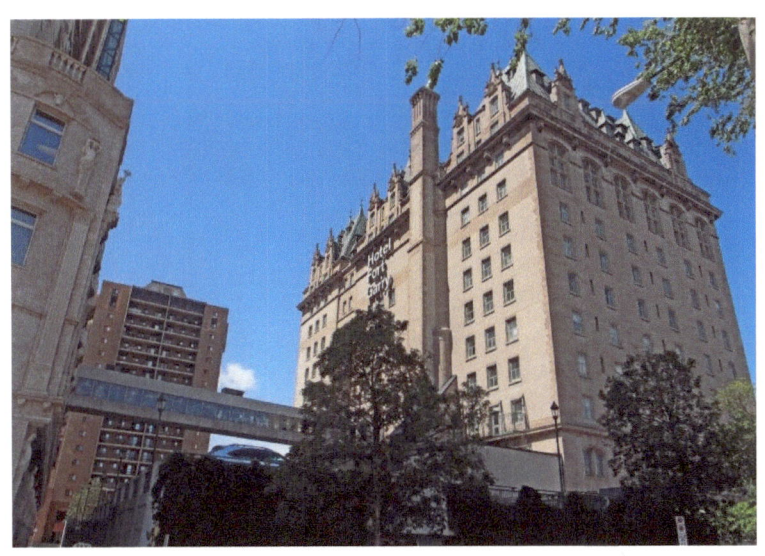

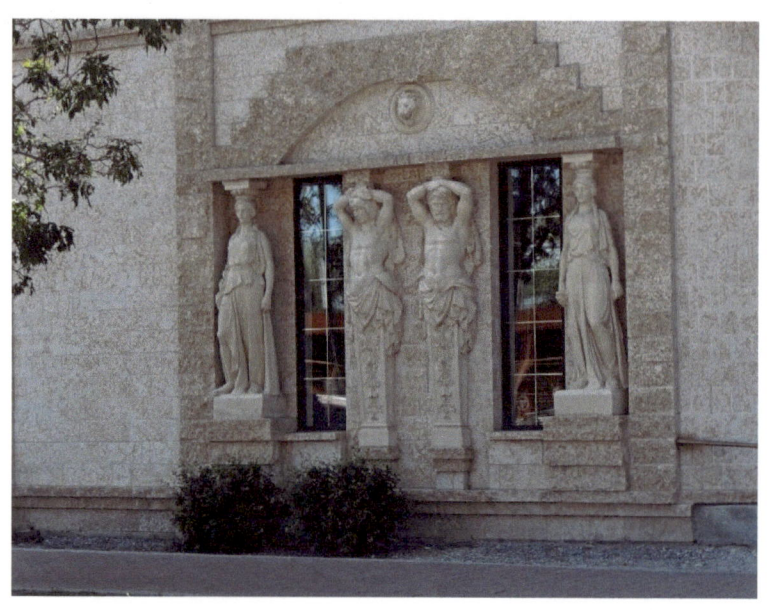

222 Broadway Avenue – Hotel Fort Garry

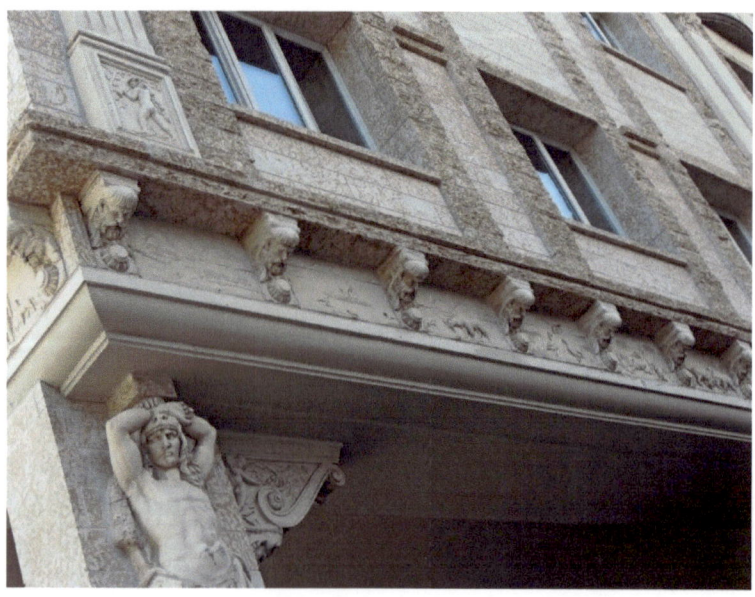

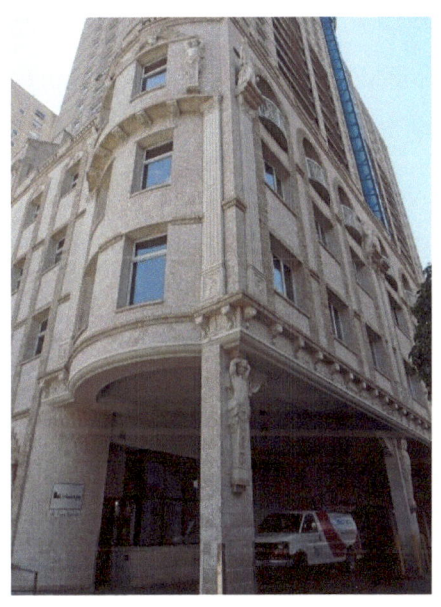

222 Broadway Avenue – Hotel Fort Garry

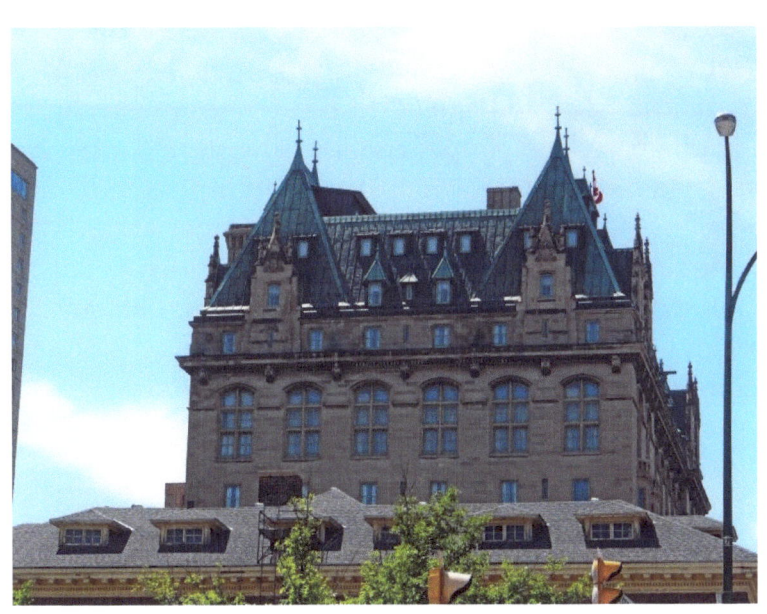

The Fort Garry Hotel is one of a series of Chateau-style hotels built by Canadian railway companies in the early twentieth century to encourage tourists to travel their transcontinental routes. Popular with the travelling public for their elaborate decor and comfortable elegance, these hotels quickly became a national symbol of quality accommodation. The Fort Garry Hotel was built in Winnipeg in 1911-13. Its Chateau style is evident in its steeply pitched, truncated hip roof punctuated by multiple peaks, progressively smaller dormer windows, and finials; its imposing massing; its smooth-cut stone cladding; and its elaborate decorative stonework. Its main block is divided into three vertical sections defined by continuous bands of string coursing and entablatures. It has a two-storey arcaded base containing the ground floor lobby and dining rooms; six intermediary storeys with a regular, alternating, window pattern; and a two-storey arcaded top containing the main reception rooms. It has strips of oriel windows flanking a slightly recessed center, delicately carved gables, Indiana limestone walls, a grey granite base; and copper roofing. The steep copper roof is defined by a multitude of small shed- and hip-roofed dormers, highly elaborate stone dormer facades at the corners, many pinnacles, and a large ornate chimney. Rich detailing is seen in the decorative stonework at the cornice, balcony balustrades atop the bay windows, and a rounded stone turret topped by a polygonal roof.

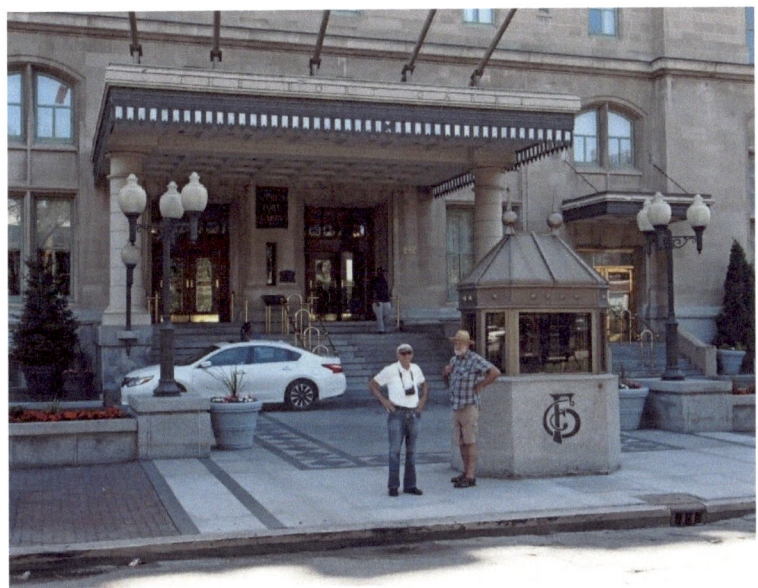

It has a formal entrance with stone stairs, brass railings, and a copper-detailed canopy. There are grand, double-height interior public spaces on the ground and seventh floors. The ground floor consists of a main lobby; a main dining room; and a circular dining room at the rear. The elaborate main lobby is surrounded by a mezzanine with four large corner piers joined by arches with keystones bearing the national or provincial emblem; a marble inlay floor; marble stairway with iron and bronze balustrade; gold-trimmed piers and moldings; bronze railing around the mezzanine; paneled ceiling; and the front desk is concealed between two pilasters. The main, two-storey dining room, occupies the length of the west side of the ground floor, and includes: large windows; marble dado; bronze sconces and chandeliers; a paneled ceiling with modeled bas-reliefs of dragons, thistles, pine cones and tulips; bronze, French doors with bronze handles ornamented with the Grand Trunk Pacific Railway (GTPR) logo.

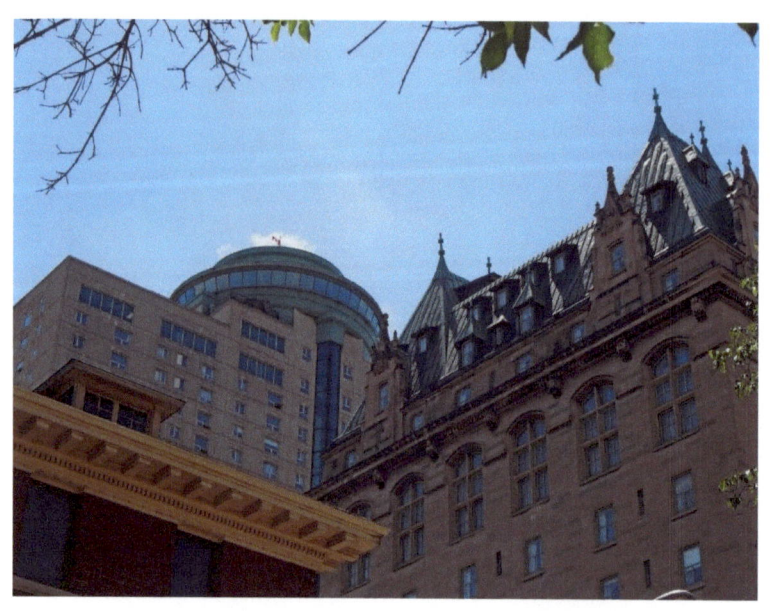

222 Broadway Avenue – Hotel Fort Garry

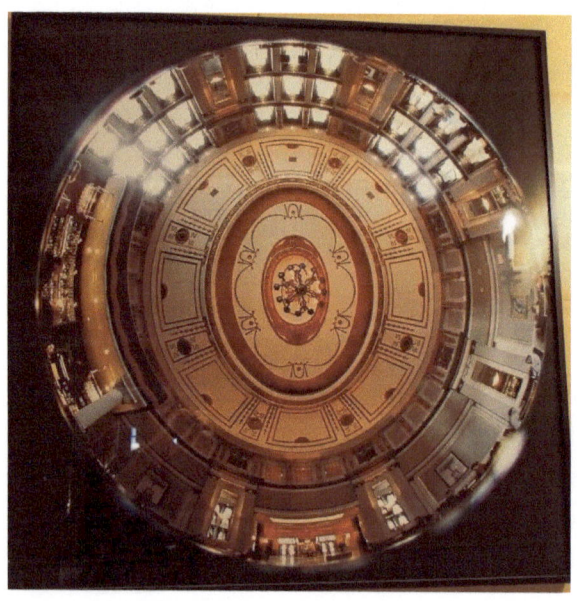

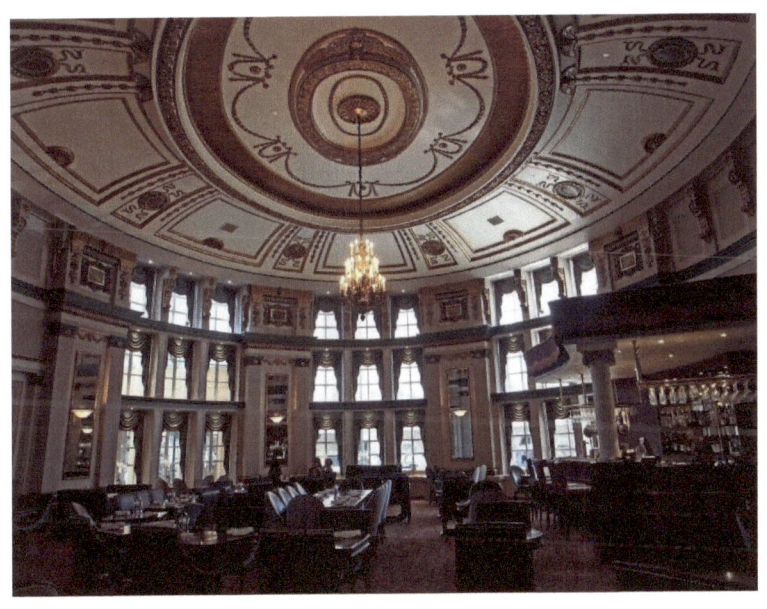

Hotel Fort Garry Main Dining Room

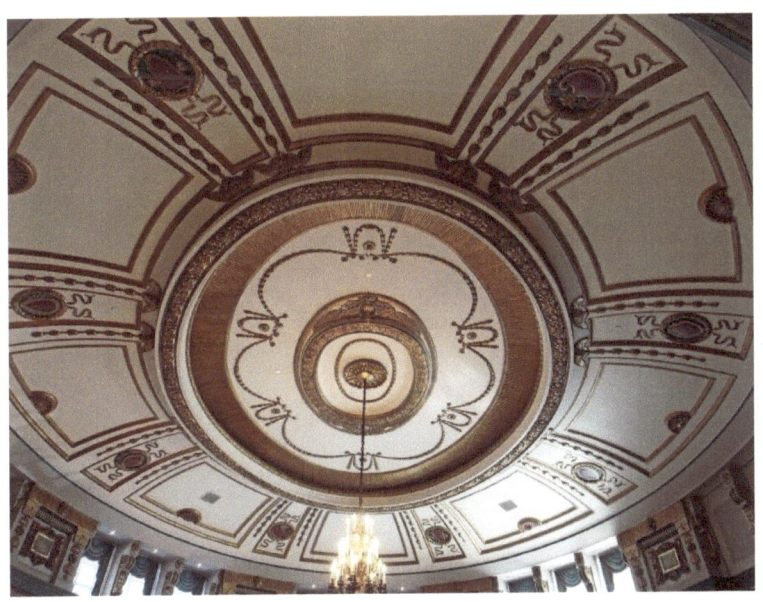

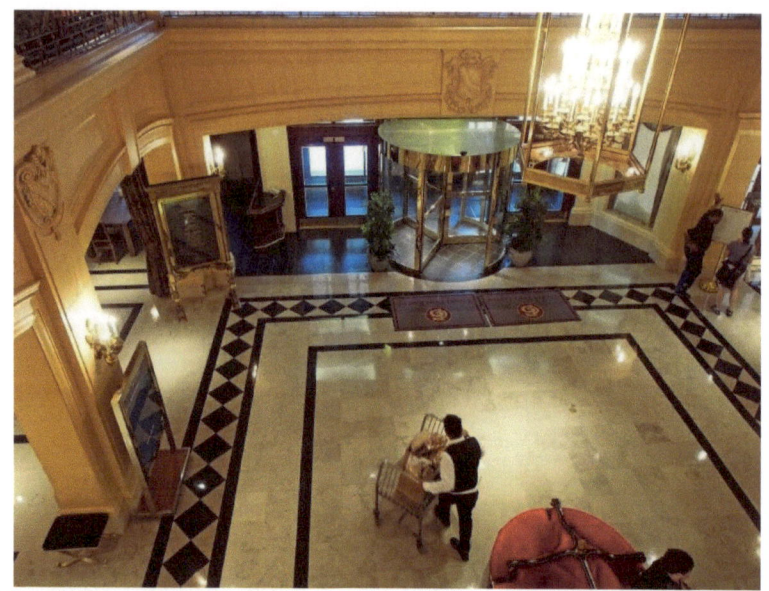

Hotel Fort Garry Main Lobby – a marble inlay floor; large corner piers joined by arches with keystones bearing the national or provincial emblem

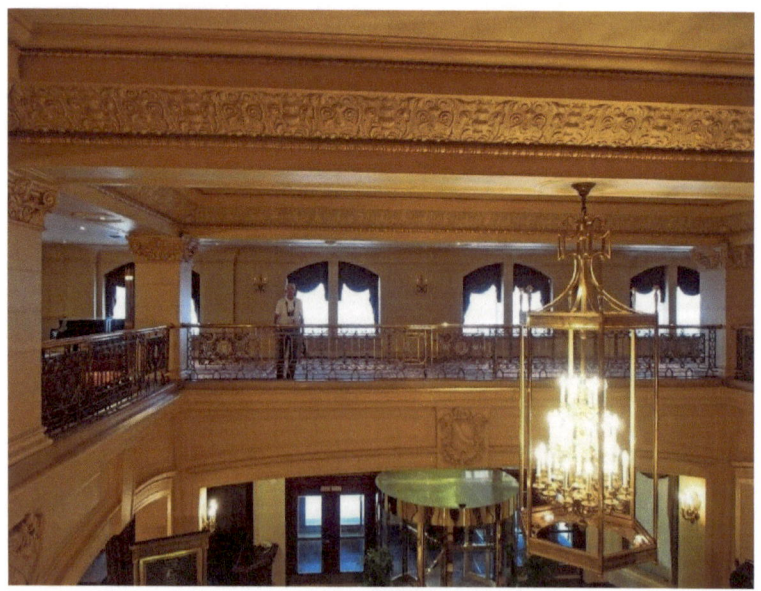

Mezzanine

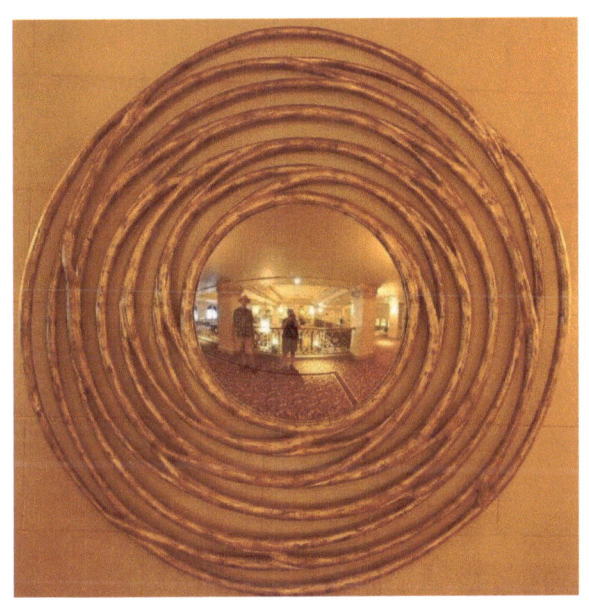

Inside Hotel Fort Garry

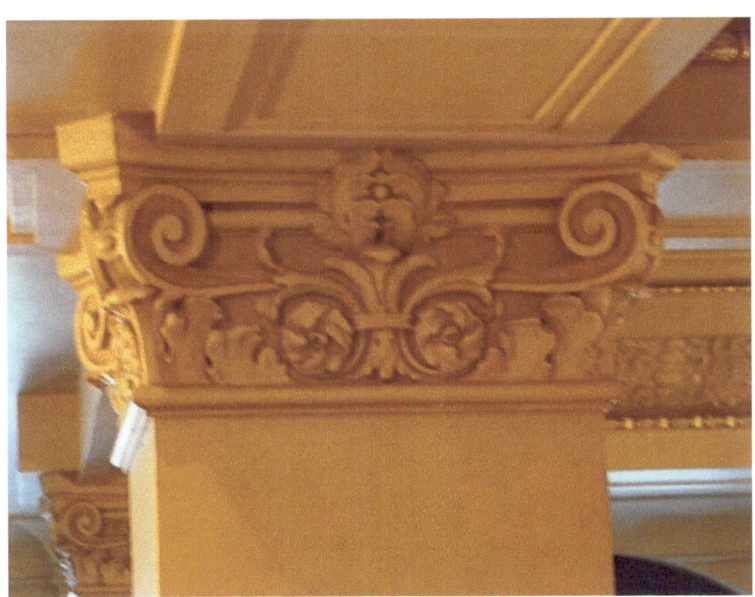

Composite Capital

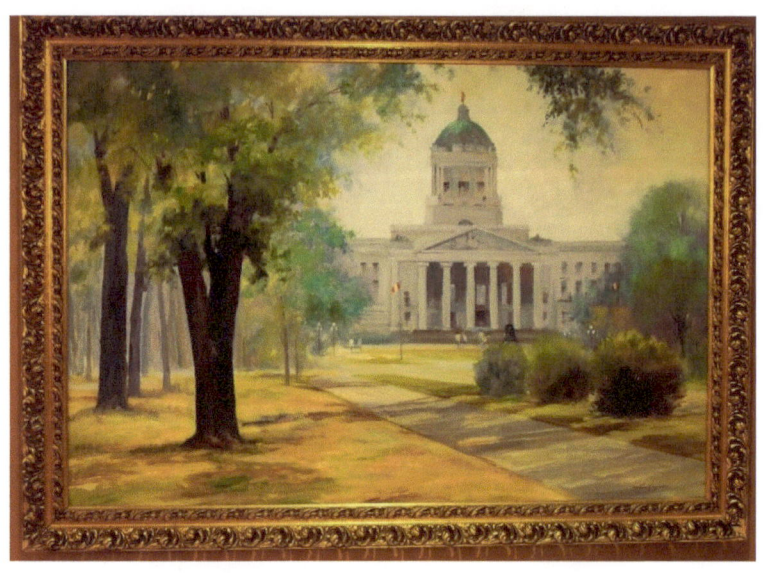

Paintings inside Hotel Fort Garry

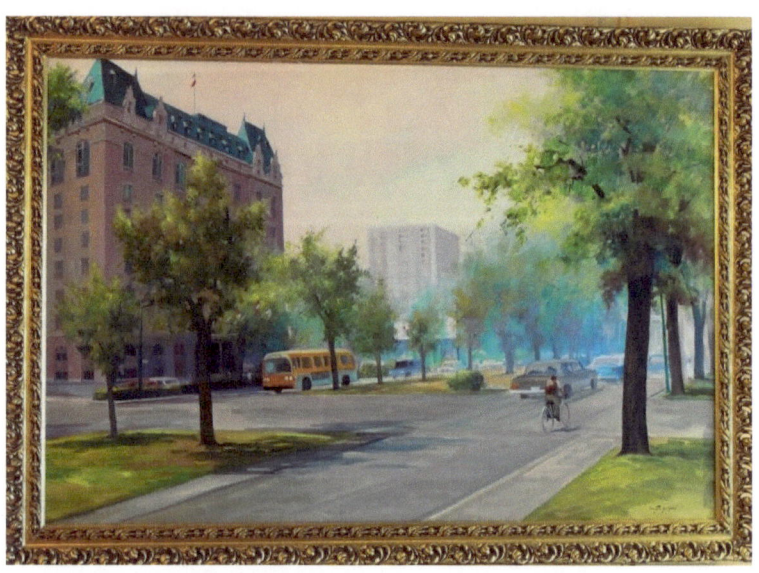

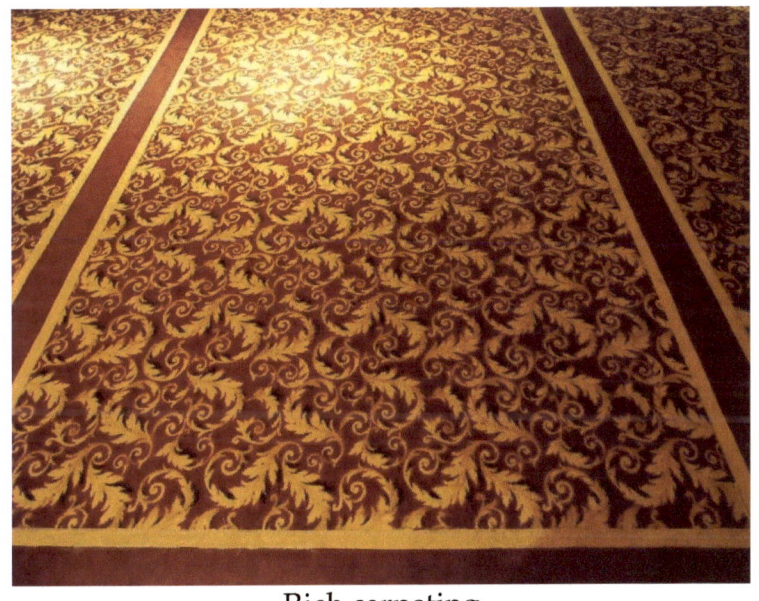

Rich carpeting

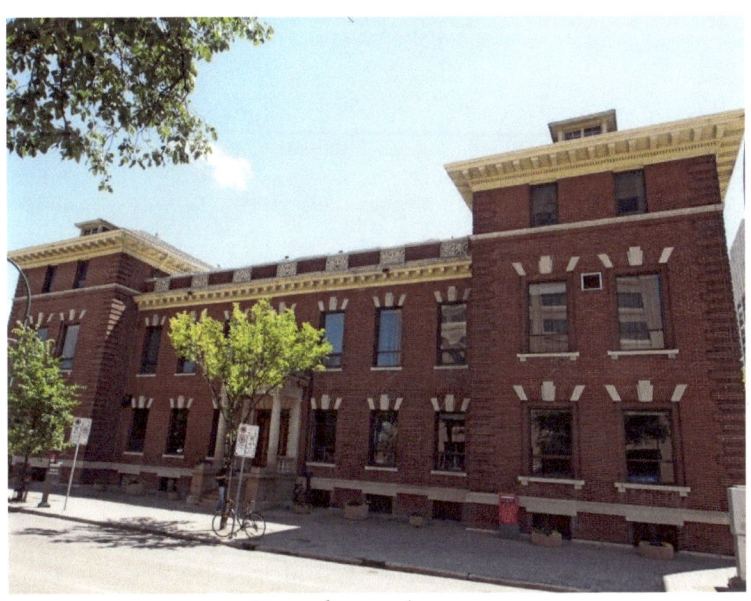

Broadway Avenue

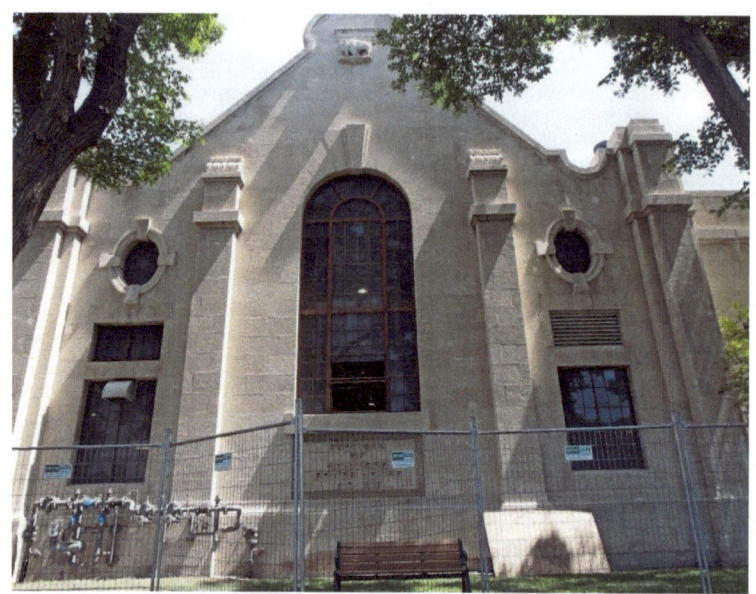

221 Memorial Boulevard – Power House A.D. 1915 – pilasters, round windows with keystones

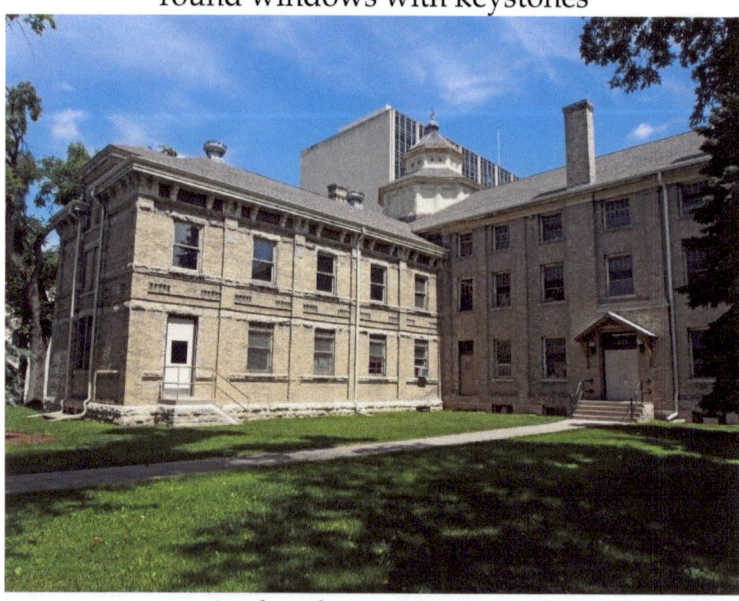

Stone courses, cornice brackets, two-storey belvedere/cupola, tall chimneys, pilasters

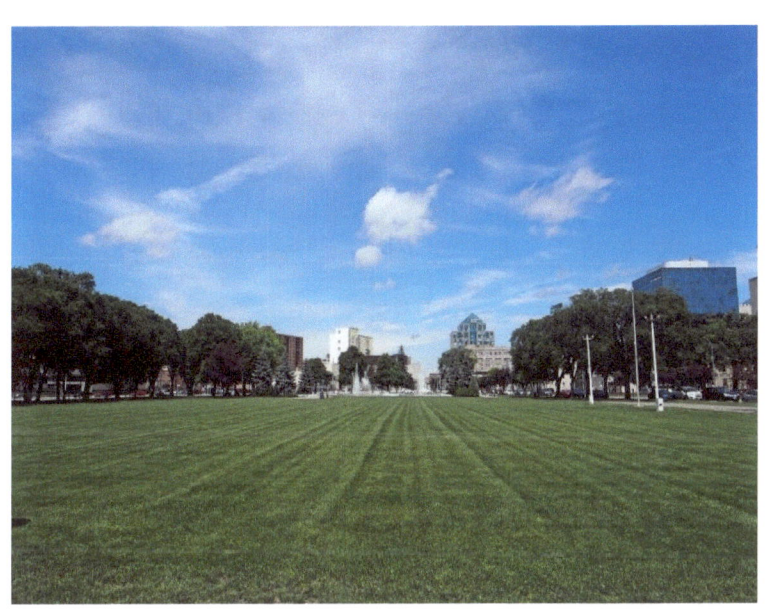

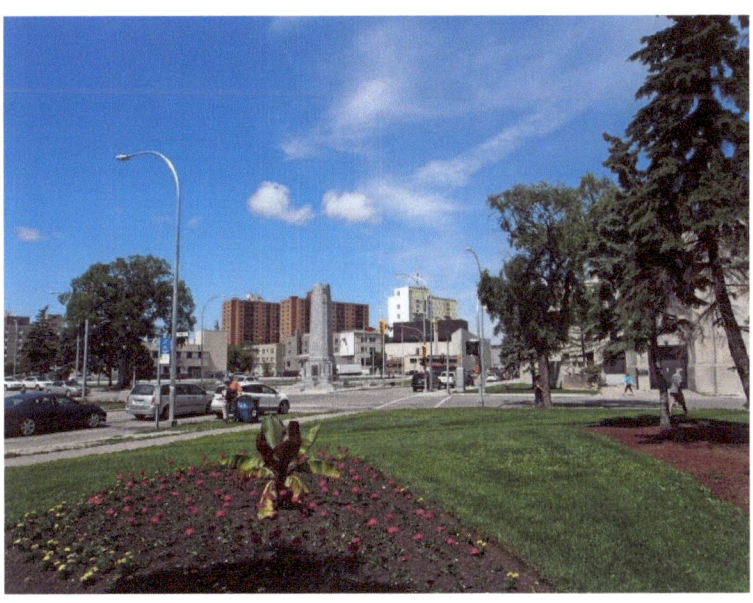

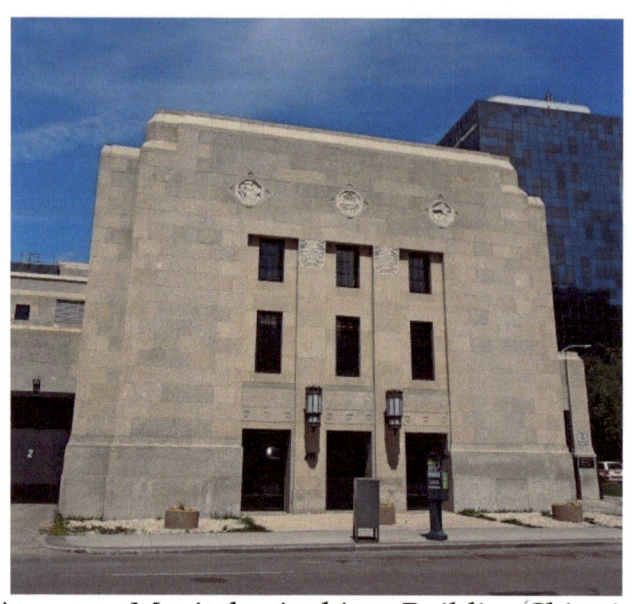

York Avenue – Manitoba Archives Building Shipping and Receiving – 1931-32 – pilasters with artistically styled capitals, decorative stone work, Manitoba crest in center with two supporting mythological warriors on either side

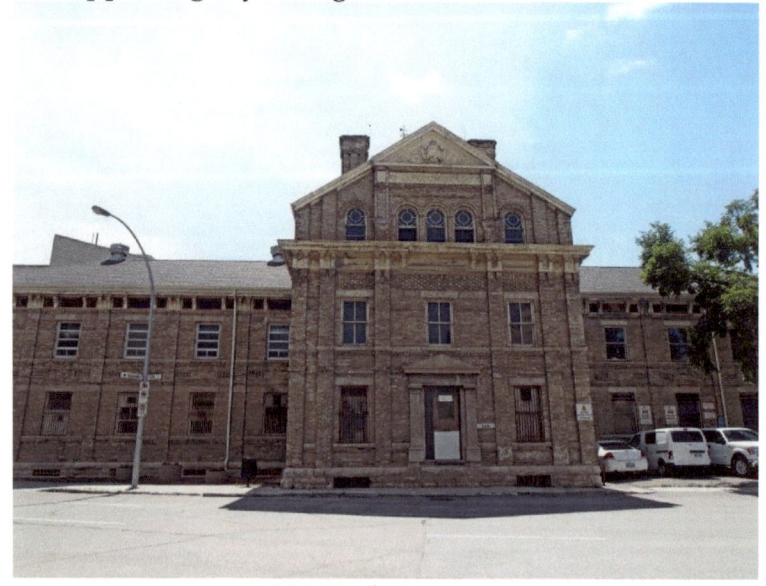

444 York Avenue

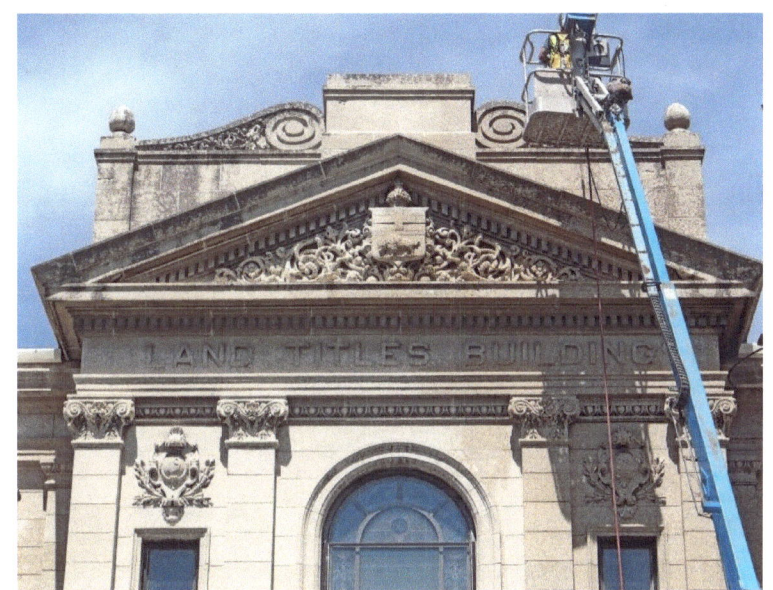

433 Broadway Avenue - Land Titles Building – cartouches 19 and 04, composite capitals on the pilasters, pediment with decorative tympanum, dentil molding, parapet

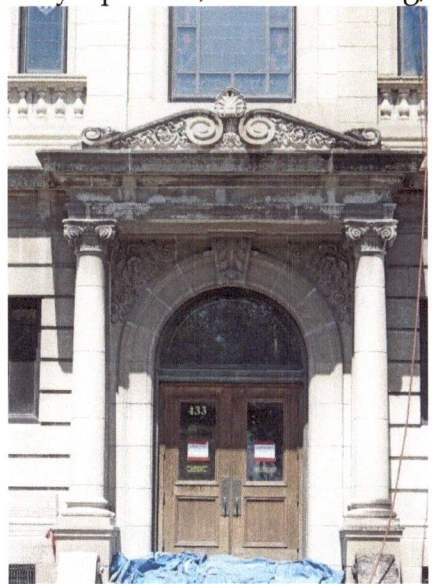

433 Broadway Avenue – Entrance – transom, door voussoirs with keystone, scrolled pediment

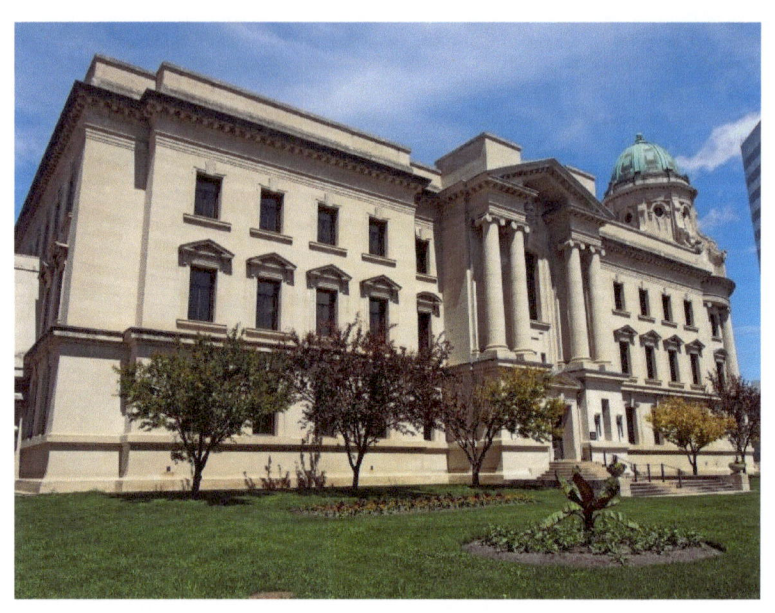

391 Broadway Avenue – Winnipeg Law Courts

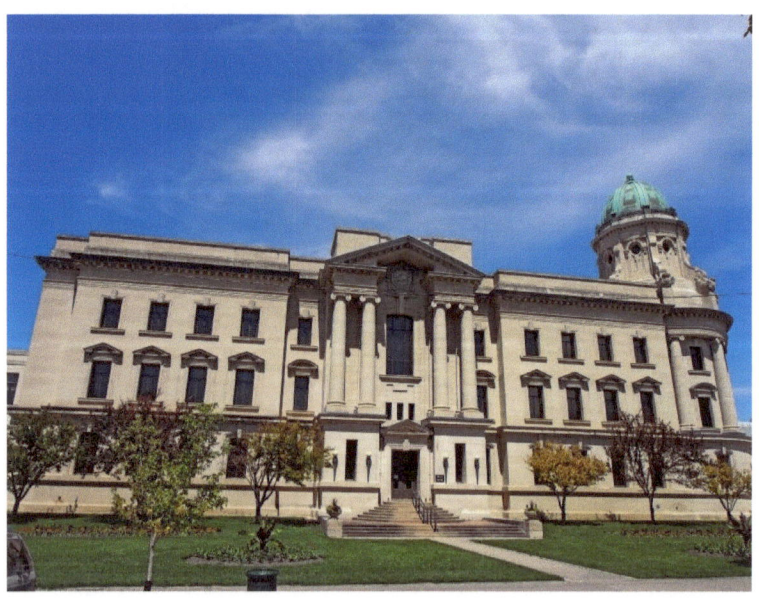

The Winnipeg Law Courts National Historic Site of Canada is located directly across from the Legislature Building in the provincial government precinct of downtown Winnipeg. It is a three-storey, Beaux Arts style building of sculpted grey limestone. Its monumental scale and prominent siting attest to its important role and symbolize the judicial institution of Manitoba. Constructed during an extended period of great optimism in the province, the Law Courts building was designed by the Provincial Architect, Victor W. Horwood, to complement the new Legislative Building, a monumental neo-classical structure under construction across the street. Beginning in 1912, construction of the steel-framed Law Courts took four years and was timed to open in conjunction with the new Legislative Building. The formal grandeur of the classically-inspired Beaux-Arts design reflects the dignity of the Law Courts. An elaborate corner cupola with a raised copper dome ties the pedimented pavilions on the south and east façades together, and draws the eye to the columned "grand entrance" on Kennedy Street. Across the façades run a dentilled cornice and a deep parapet, all in creamy-grey limestone. Interior court rooms feature large windows, with the higher courts accessed by interior passageways so that prisoners could be brought directly into the court from holding areas below, and to provide private entries for the judges.

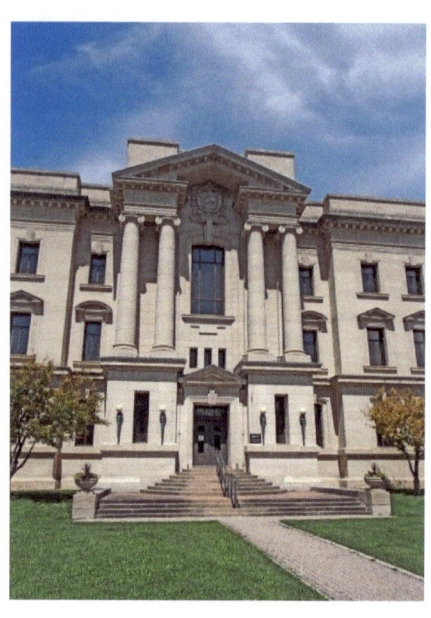

Two-storey Ionic pillars supporting an open pediment with
the Manitoba crest inside

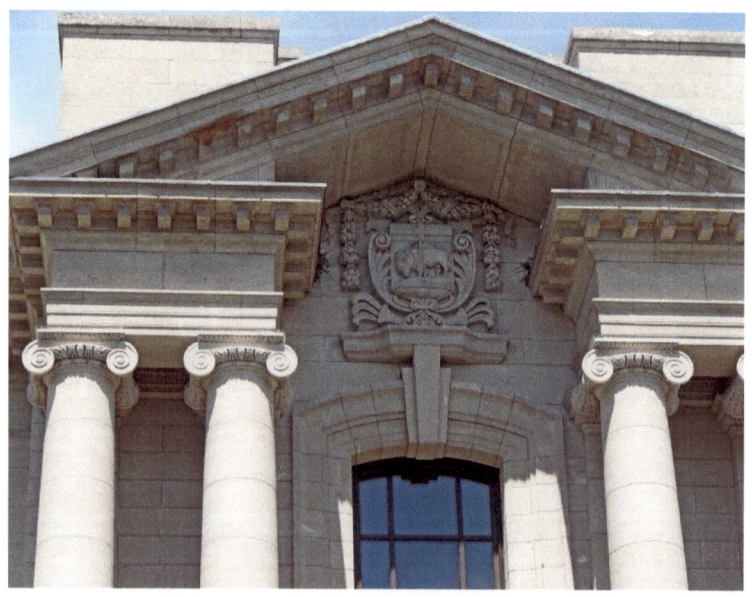

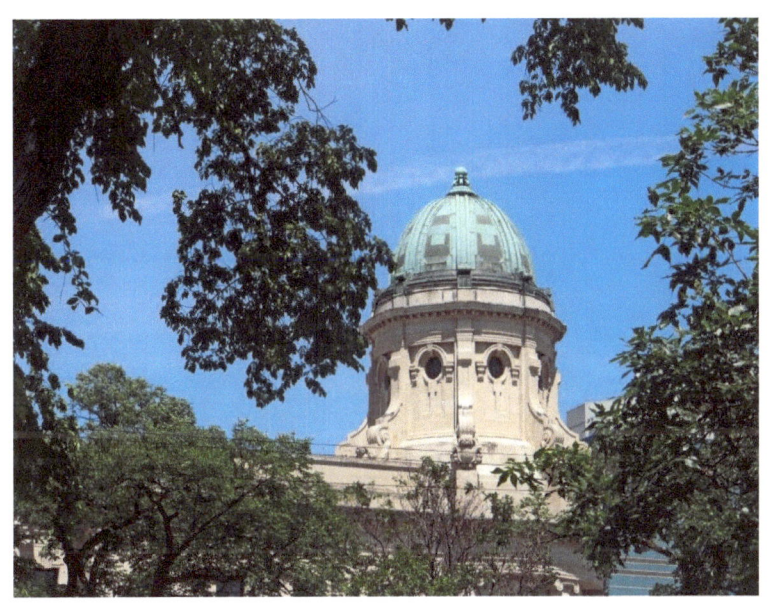

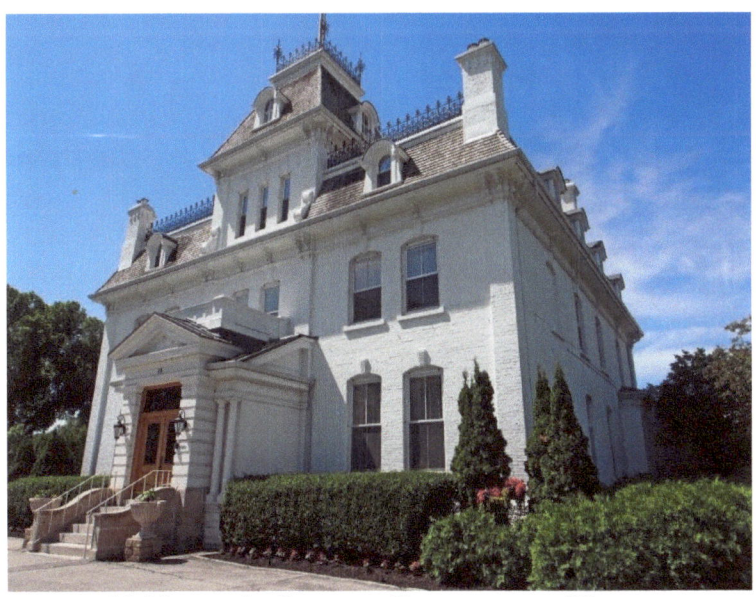

10 Kennedy Street – Government House

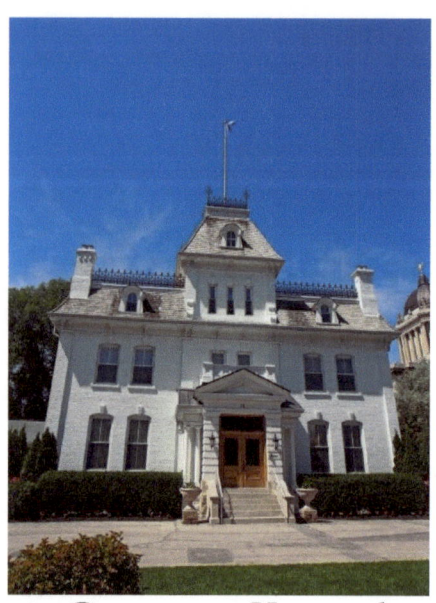

10 Kennedy Street – Government House - the official residence of the Lieutenant-Governor of Manitoba – completed in 1883

Manitoba's Government house is a structure of solid masonry walls and timber floor framing. It is Second Empire architecture with a flat steep-side mansard roof with dormers. The royal bedroom on the second floor is reserved for use by the sovereign and other Royal Family members when they are in Winnipeg, and the gold room accommodates royal support staff or other royals if the monarch is occupying the royal bedroom. The attic floor has been divided into four bedrooms, two bathrooms, a sitting room, and a three and one-half room suite for the resident housekeeper. From this floor the tower can be accessed. The lieutenant governor's standard is flown when he or she is in residence.

Manitoba's Government House is surrounded on three sides by manicured gardens. In 2010, part of the grounds was dedicated as the *Queen Elizabeth II Gardens* by the Queen on July 3 that year, in preparation for the Queen's Diamond Jubilee in 2012. At the same time, a statue of The Queen that had been created in 1970 by Leo Mol was moved here and unveiled by the Queen.

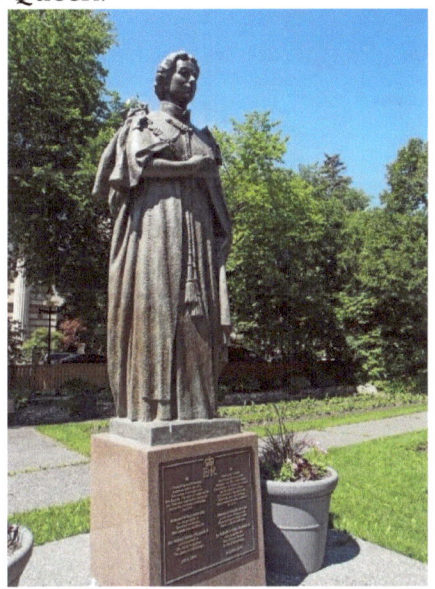

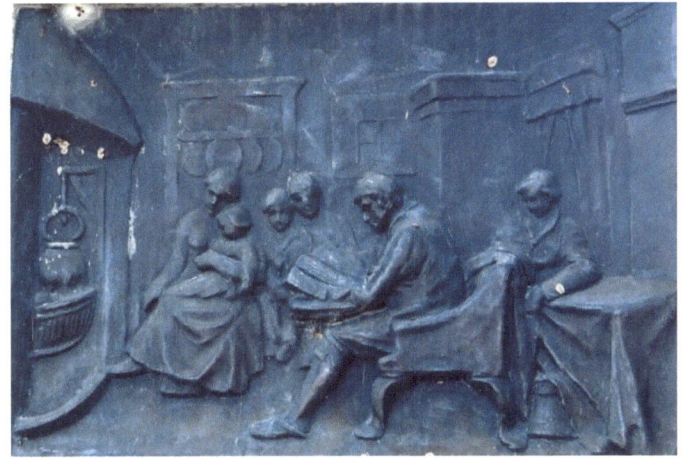

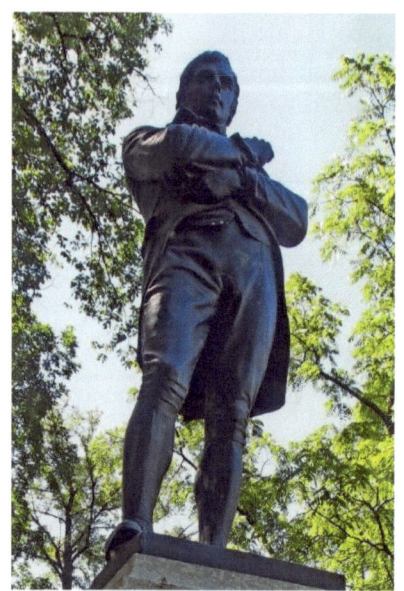

Robert Burns – 1759-1796

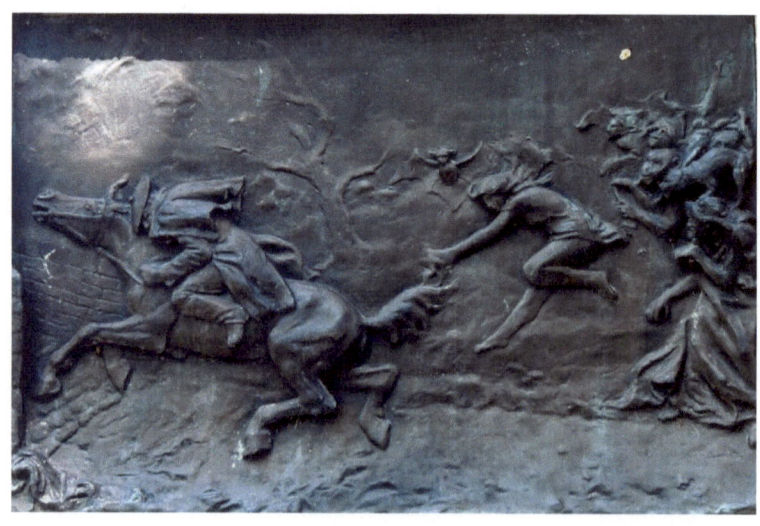

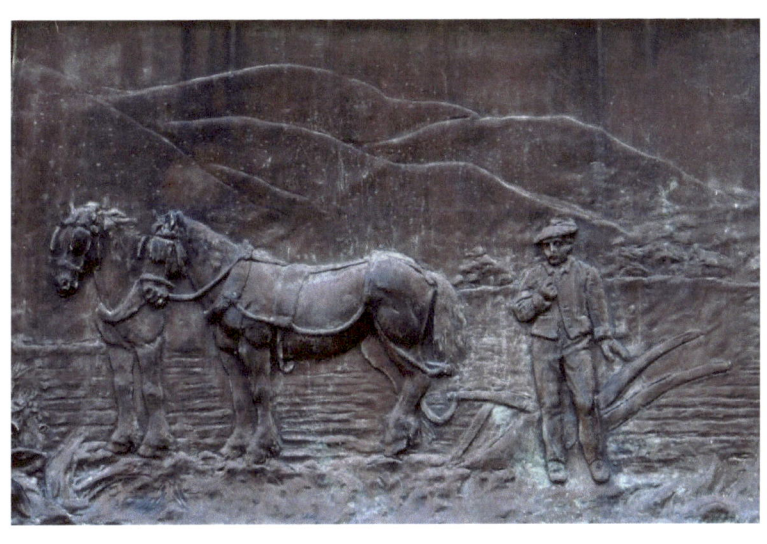

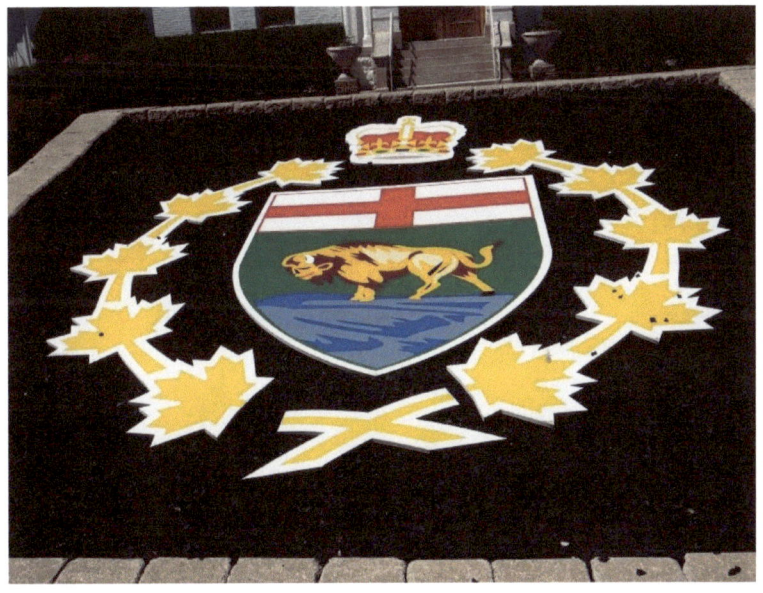

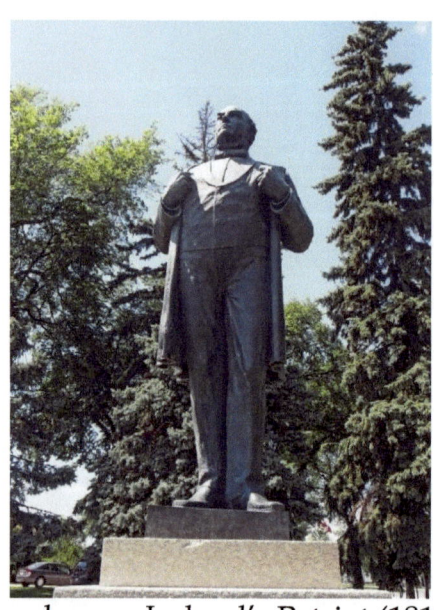

Jon Sigurdsson – Iceland's Patriot (1811-1879)

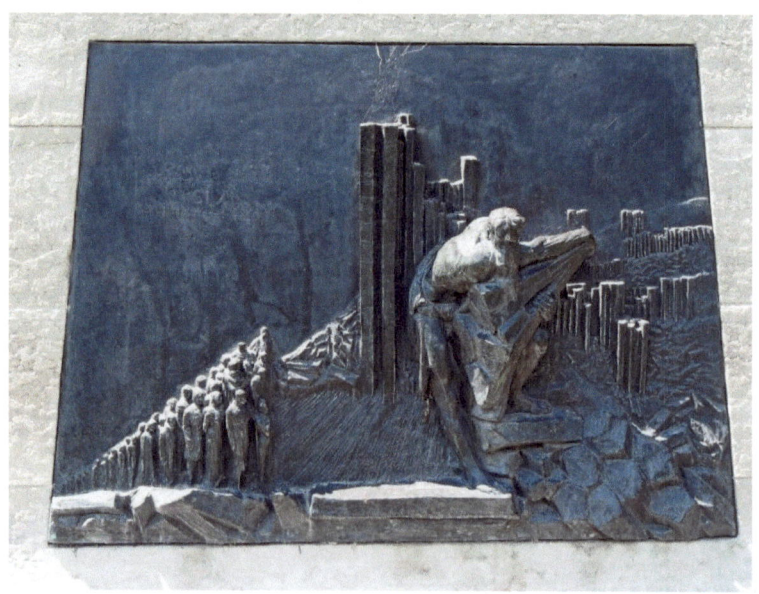

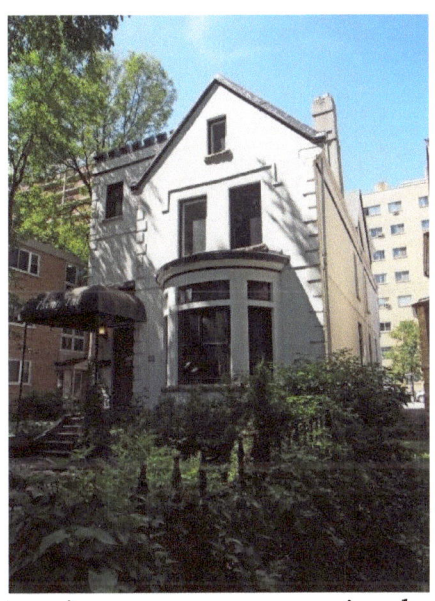

22 Edmonton Avenue – corner quoins, bay window

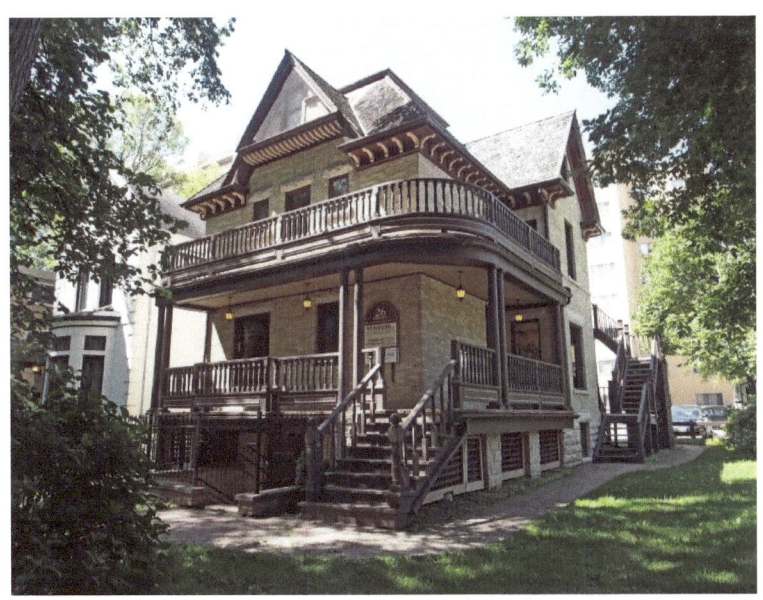

26 Edmonton Avenue – cornice brackets, two-storey
wraparound verandas

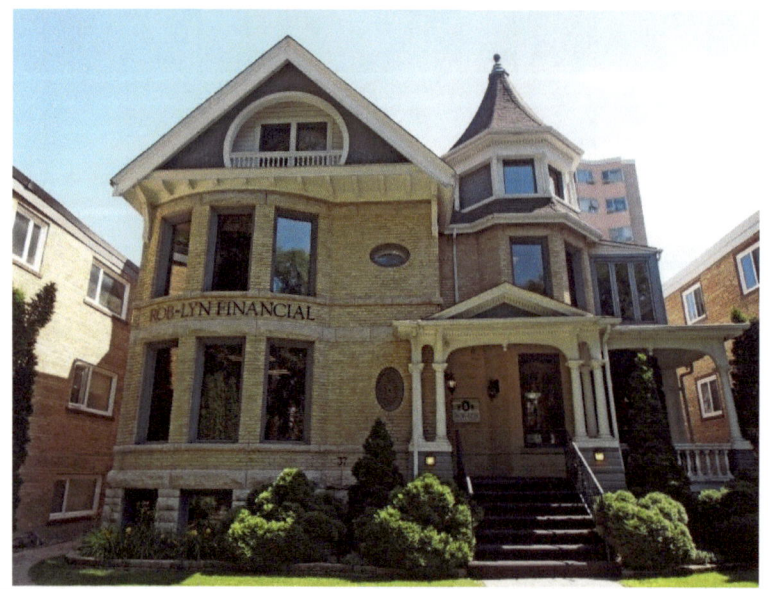

37 Edmonton Avenue – Queen Anne style, turret, veranda with Doric pillars, pediment, two-storey bay window

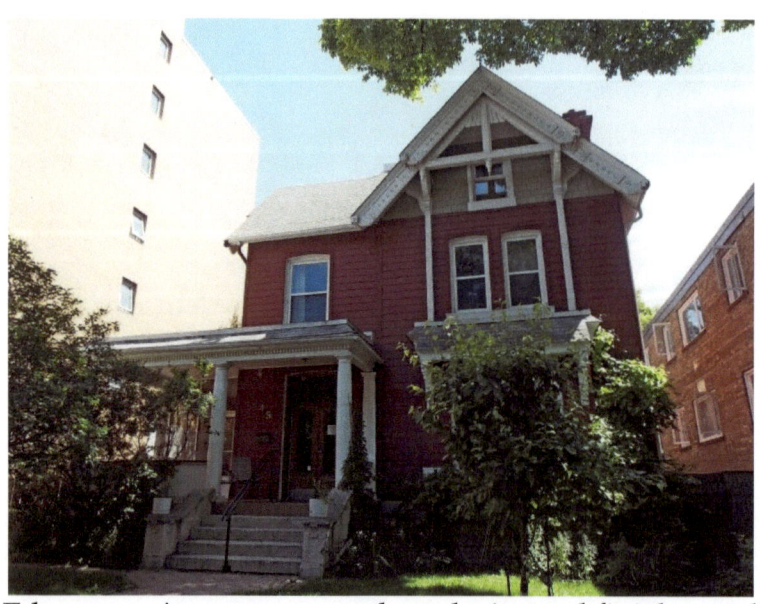

45 Edmonton Avenue – verge board trim and finial on gable, fretwork, veranda with Doric pillars

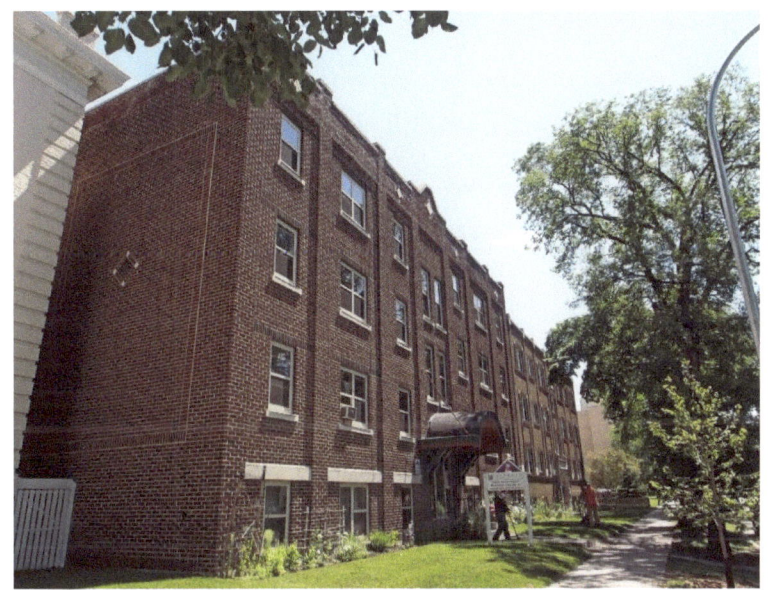

75 Edmonton Avenue – Willingdon Apartments – pilasters, stepped pediment at roofline

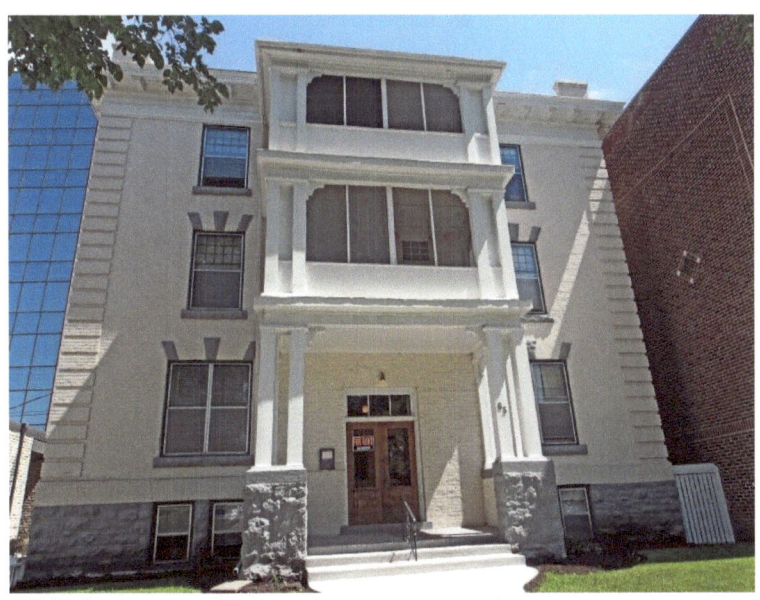

85 Edmonton Avenue – corner quoins, voussoirs over windows, three-storey pillared porches

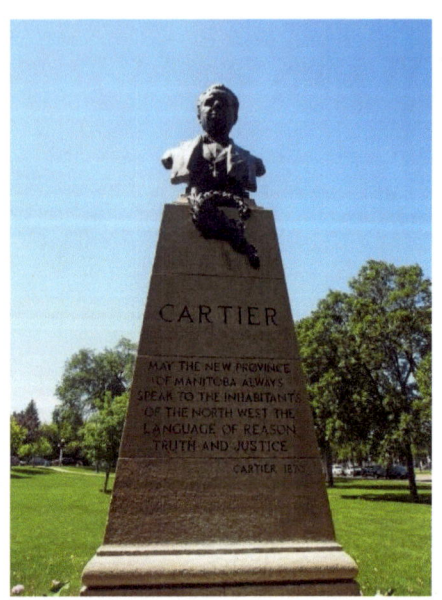

Cartier

May the new province of Manitoba always speak to the
inhabitants of the northwest the language of reason, truth and
justice   Cartier - 1870

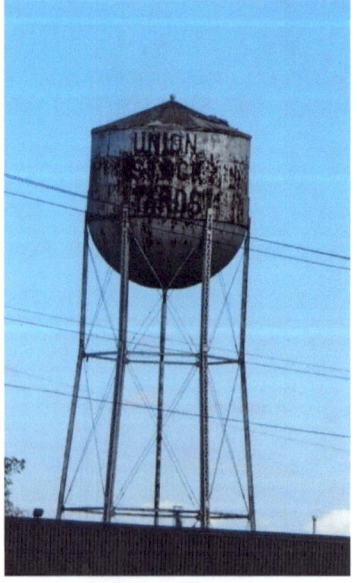

Water Tower

Architectural Terms

Balustrade: A railing system, generally around a balcony or on a second level, consisting of balusters and a top rail Example: 314 Broadway Avenue, Page 6	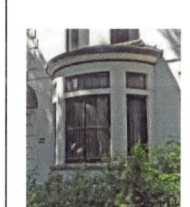
Bay Window: A window that projects out from a wall, in a semicircular, rectangular, or polygonal design. Used frequently in Gothic and Victorian designs. Example: 22 Edmonton Avenue, Page 51	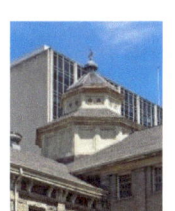
Belvedere: (from the Italian "beautiful view") an architectural feature on a roof, in a garden or on a terrace that gives a beautiful view. Example: 221 Memorial Boulevard, Page 38	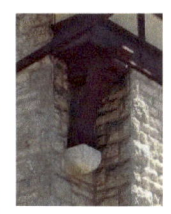
Brackets: a decorative or weight-bearing structural element which forms a right angle with one side against a wall and the other under a projecting surface such as an eave or roof. Example: 529 Wellington Crescent, Page 6	

Capital: The uppermost finish or decoration on a column. An Ionic column has a small base, a thin elegant shaft, and a capital composed of volutes which are carved whirls or twists that take the form of a scroll.
Example: 450 Broadway Avenue, Page 10

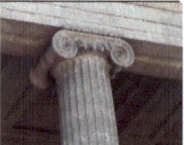

Ionic

A Doric column is characterized by a plain column with no base, a shaft with twenty flutings, and a simple capital with a simple entablature. Example: 37 Edmonton Avenue , Page 52

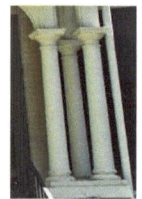

Doric

A Corinthian column is characterized by a rounded capital decorated with acanthus leaves and a square abacus (the uppermost portion of a capital directly below the entablature) on tall slender columns.
Example: 450 Broadway Avenue, Page 10

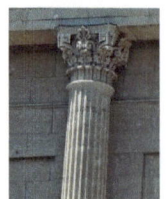

Corinthian

A Composite is a mixture of two or sometimes, three, of the major styles listed above.
Example: 222 Broadway Avenue, Page 35

Composite

Cartouche: Taken from the French name for a scroll of paper, this is an ornament from the late Renaissance or Baroque era that bears the name of the building's patron on a paper with rolled up edges.
Example: 433 Broadway Avenue, Page 41

Cornice: originally the wooden overhang of the roof. With the use of stone, brick, iron and steel, the cornice is any horizontal moulded projection at the top of a building. They can be very decorative. Example: 450 Broadway Avenue, Page 7	
Cupola: A domed or curved roof rising from a building as a decorative element. Example: 450 Broadway Avenue, Page 9	
Dentil Moulding: an even series of rectangles used as ornamental decoration in cornices. Example: 450 Broadway Avenue, Page 9	
Dome: Any roof structure that is curved and spans an ultimately circular base. Squinches and pendentives are used to provide a circular base on a square or rectilinear tower. A squinch is a construction filling in the upper angles of a square room so as to form a base to receive an octagonal **or** spherical dome. When a square space is vaulted to provide a circular space for a dome the resulting curved triangular supports are called pendentives. This is most common in Byzantine architecture. Example: 433 Broadway Avenue, Page 41	

Dormer: (French for "sleep") a gable end window that pierces through the plane of a sloping roof surface to create usable space in the top floor or attic of a building by adding headroom. Example: 10 Kennedy Street, Page 45	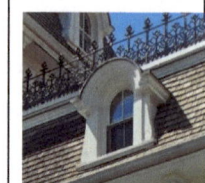
Entrance: The entrance encompasses the doorway and the inner vestibule or, in residential architecture, the covered porch. Example: 450 Broadway Avenue, Page 9	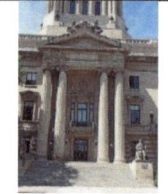
Gable: the triangular portion of a wall between the edges of a sloping roof. Example: 222 Broadway Avenue, Page 29	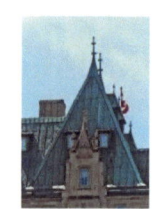
Iron Cresting: A decorative ornament along the top of a roof. Iron cresting was popular in the Baroque era and also in Italianate, Victorian, Second Empire and Queen Anne styles of architecture. Example: 10 Kennedy Street, Page 45	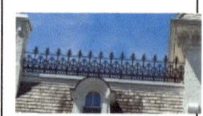
Keystones and Voussoirs: a voussoir is a wedge-shaped element used in building an arch. A keystone is the central stone that locks all the stones into position, allowing the arch to bear weight. A keystone is often enlarged and embellished. Example: 221 Memorial Boulevard, Page 38	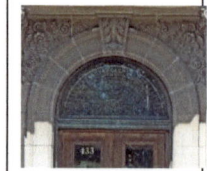

Muntin: When a window unit has more than one pane, the material that separates the panes is called the muntin. The larger, more decorative separations are called mullions. In stained glass windows, each piece of colored glass is held in place by a muntin. These were traditionally made of iron. Example: 499 Broadway Avenue, Page 21	
Parapet: low wall around the edge of a roof. Example: 222 Broadway Avenue, Page 26	
Pediment: a triangular section above the door or portico, usually supported by columns. The inside of the triangle is called the tympanum. Example: 450 Broadway Avenue, Page 7	
Pilaster: a slightly projecting column built into or applied to the face of a wall for additional structural support. Example: 433 Broadway Avenue, Page 41	
Quoin: masonry blocks at the corner of a wall, often a decorative feature, usually larger or of a different colour than the rest of the wall. Example: 85 Edmonton Avenue, Page 53	

Tower: A circular, square, or octagonal vertical structure higher than the surrounding structure that is usually part of an existing building and is created either for extra defense or for a specific purpose such as a clock or a bell tower. Example: 545 Broadway Avenue, Page 25	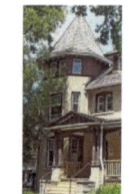
Transom Window: the light above the doorway, also called a fanlight. Example: 433 Broadway Avenue, Page 41	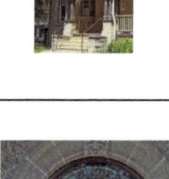
Verge board and Finial: also called bargeboards – hang from the projecting end of a roof and are often elaborately carved and ornamented. **Finial:** ornament added to the top of a gable, pinnacle, canopy or spire – a Gothic element. Example: 45 Edmonton Avenue, Page 52	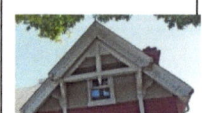

Building Styles

Beaux Arts: Promoters of this style sought to express the classical principles on a grand and imposing scale. Many of the Beaux Arts buildings were banks, post offices, and railway stations. The Ontario Beaux Arts style is eclectic mixing elements of Classical, Renaissance and Baroque. Often the designs have a temple-like façade, porticos with pediments, balustrades, and capitals in many styles. Example: 450 Broadway Avenue, Page 9	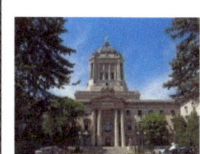
Gothic Revival, 1830-1890 – These decorative buildings have sharply-pitched gables with highly detailed verge boards, pointed-arch window openings, and dichromatic brickwork. It is a common style in Ontario. Example: 499 Broadway Avenue, Page 21	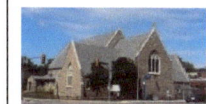
Greek Revival – have gabled or hipped roofs with low pitches. The cornice of the main roof usually has a wide band which represents the entablature of classical Greek architecture consisting of the frieze and the architrave. Greek or Roman columns usually support the porch. The front door is surrounded by sidelights and a rectangular transom and is usually dressed with pilasters, pediments and/or columns. Example: 450 Broadway Avenue, Page 7	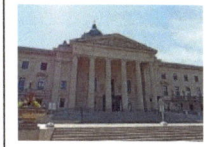

Neo-Georgian architecture seeks to revive elements of architectural style of American colonial architecture of the period around the Revolutionary War which drew strongly from Georgian architecture of Great Britain. Architecture from the 18th and early 19th centuries in Ontario includes a wide assortment of detailing and ornament applied to a design centered around the fireplace and the source of water. Structures typically have a symmetrical front facade with elaborate front doorways, often with decorative crown pediments, fanlights, and sidelights, symmetrical windows flanking the front entrance and columned porches. Example: 177 Colony Street, Page 23	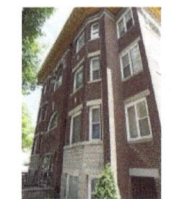
Queen Anne, 1885-1900 – This style is distinguished by an irregular outline featuring a combination of an offset tower, broad gables, projecting two-storey bays, verandahs, multi-sloped roofs, and tall, decorative chimneys. A mixture of brick and wood is common. Windows often have one large single-paned bottom sash and small panes in the upper sash. Example: 37 Edmonton Avenue, Page 52	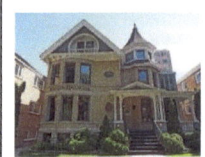
Second Empire, 1860-1880 – The mansard roof is the most noteworthy feature of this style and is evidence of the French origins. Projecting central towers and one or two-storey bays can also be present. Example: 10 Kennedy Street, Page 46	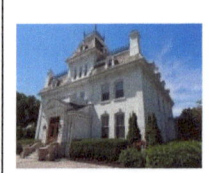